T0114167

BUDDY REMEMBERS - THEN AND NOW

A PERSONAL HISTORY OF MY PARENTS' LIVES

JOSEPH N. MUZIO
WRITTEN 2005-2008

Order this book online at www.trafford.com
or email orders@trafford.com

Most Trafford titles are also available at major online book retailers.

Print information available on the last page.

ISBN: 978-1-4251-6510-9 (sc)
ISBN: 978-1-4269-9132-5 (e)

Trafford rev. 04/02/2019

 www.trafford.com

North America & international
toll-free: 1 888 232 4444 (USA & Canada)
fax: 812 355 4082

THINGS ARE NEVER THE WAY THEY SEEM.
ROBERT F. MURPHY (deceased 1990)

DEDICATIONS AND ACKNOWLEDGEMENTS:

THIS memoir is dedicated to Phyllis Brancata Muzio and Frank Muzio, my long deceased parents who still live spiritually within me. I think of them every day if only for a moment. To my wife Lois Ann Grant Muzio who encouraged me to persevere, never doubting this writing project. She believed in me then, and now. She read it with a critical and analytical eye, listened, asked questions, offered suggestions and contributed with significant comments and improvements. She gave me her support with her usual grace, care and persuasion. Our youngest son Matthew also offered insightful suggestions, often finding connections I had somehow missed.

I also dedicate this book to our three sons, Frank Paul, Edward Victor and Matthew Phillip, and to our two grandchildren, Mia Frank and Joseph Grant, within whom those mysterious and inherited fragments of Phyllis and Frank's DNA exist. They can only benefit from knowing more about the lives of their ancestors. To my second cousins Mildred Buono D'Eri and Henry Buono Jr. who helped me piece together the scant and scattered information about my father's early years. Their grandfather Joseph was my father's older brother and the person I was named after. To my loving Aunt Rose, the surviving sister of the four Brancata women, who provided information about my mother and their family and with whom she was so close throughout their lives.

To my dear friend Joe Kinneary for his integrity and perseverance, whose memoir writing helped me to better understand who he is and what is involved in this kind of writing. Joe and his wife Nancy read a draft of this book and provided comments.

To my deceased dear friend Bob Murphy whose conversations and writings many years ago instilled in me the courage to write this memoir. Bob was a gifted thinker, writer and scholar.

To the remaining members of the Muzio and Brancata families who originally came to the United States with virtually nothing and worked hard to create productive lives for themselves and their offspring.

To all who spoke to me about this writing project, listened to me, or made comments. To those mentioned by name or inference, I hope they are neither offended nor gratified by my perceptions and forthrightness.

To my friend and former colleague Shelly Friedland, who voluntarily provided his computer expertise, advice and time so my book could effectively be formatted and then electronically prepared for the publisher. Shelly also improved the quality of the family pictures in this book.

To Richard A. Danca, my editor, who professionally and expeditiously brought a sharper directness to my writing. He also encouraged me to consider removing and/or markedly reducing some topical digressions. Earlier drafts of the book were almost a 100 pages more. This included a chapter about major modern societal issues, especially exponential human population growth coupled with chronic environmental abuses, exploitations of natural resources, insatiable materialism, and the connectedness between corruption and greed. In my early enthusiasm of this writing, I became involved in an intellectual frenzy, twisting and tearing about topics that are not related to my parents. Earlier, when they read a draft, both Lois and Matthew made comments similar to Richard's. Our other sons Frank and Edward independently came to this conclusion too. All of these concerned individuals certainly couldn't be wrong. They helped me to be far more singularly focused on my primary mission. Those other vital matters rightfully belong in a separate future project. Considering them in this memoir would have only diluted and detracted.

I also want to thank the caring and competent educators who so many years ago exposed me to scholarship, newer knowledge, and ways of thinking at Columbia, especially chemistry professors Larkin Farinholt and Charles Dawson, philosophy professor Irwin Edman, health education professor James Malfetti, art professor Rice, physical education professor and former All-American football player at Columbia Paul Governali, and my academic advisor Gordon Ridings, who was also the varsity basketball coach.

There were fine professors at Queens College who also guided me and helped me to become a clearer thinker and a more inquisitive person, especially biology professors Donald E. Lancefield, and Drs. Colwin, political science professor Mary Earhart Dillon, physical education professor Al Feld, and several English professors who increased my appreciation for the written word in different time periods, places and forms.

Finally, especially to those who call themselves writers, I now realize first-hand the depth and breadth of their struggles to be truthful in their creations. Throughout my teenage and adult years, I had written all sorts of papers in college and graduate school; investigative reports and other legal documents as a United States Marine Corps officer; a doctoral thesis; evaluations of colleagues; and grant proposals. I also published scientific research papers and academic journal articles; co-authored two scholarly books in the biological sciences; and written many academic book reviews.

This memoir project was remarkably different than any of these writing activities. It is my sole effort to write an introspective and reflective personal memoir about the lives of my parents and their children. As I became immersed in it, this process became more intensely complicated, while growing almost organically. For me, it became simultaneously an exhausting and exhilarating journey, in some respects, similar to successfully climbing to the pinnacle of Mount Everest and then descending back to ground level. One Everest climber remarked: "To climb to the summit is optional, to climb back down is compulsory."

CHAPTER I

WHY TAKE THIS JOURNEY NOW?

How can I compare writing about my parents, Phyllis and Frank Muzio with the first successful climbing and descending of Mount Everest by Edmund Hillary and Tenzing Norgay on May 29th 1953, or even the failed attempts by George Mallory many years before? I have thought about this journey for a long time, am finally embarking upon it, determined to finish it. Admittedly, it is nowhere as dangerous or as arduous as climbing Mount Everest. Nor is it comparable to any human adventure testing my physical and mental abilities, and endurance.

Why am I writing about my parents now, so many years after they died? In 1924 Mallory famously said he continued to make efforts to successfully climb Everest (which he never did) "because it's there," and I feel the same about my parents' story: They were here. They lived. They were the most significant people in my life and my sister's, and to some beyond us. I want others to know about them. It's important to share the details and memories of their lives, their very existences, with our family and others. Maybe if the children of all those other parents have the time, energy and commitment, they too could write their recollections about their parents. How else will we know about all those who were here and carried out their daily chores, loved, provided strength and ongoing efforts to their children and their grandchildren, their neighbors, took their places in a broader community? They are part of humanity's collective forces.

This is a lengthy treatment of my parents' life histories, some of their memorable days and events, and my perceptions of them. This memoir will confirm that their lives were inexorably intertwined with lives of their children, and their relatives, and on occasion to seemingly unrelated topics. There's no need to apologize for any of this, and yet I inexplicably find myself apologizing in advance. What is here is thoroughly mine. I accept full responsibility for it, including any warts or disappointments to others. If I have failed anybody beside myself, I offer my apologies right at the beginning.

Writing can be rigorous, sometimes lonely and exhausting. Though it lacks those treacherous and unknown aspects of climbing Mount Everest in certain ways my journey may take on the unknown and become a little treacherous. My exploration has challenging aspects, even though it is exclusively explorations within my mind, remembrances and emotions. As I go about recalling and examining years-ago matters, this journey has encouraged me to delve into memory recesses and crevices, long-buried neuronal connections, and those forgotten past events and feelings. It has taken me on some roads and paths that it might have been better to avoid. Also, now that I'm well down the road of my life, I call this "on the other side of the mountain," I have tried to provide some introspective interpretation of these recollected matters.

Some of these recollections may be out of sequence, or be partially inaccurate recreations. Then again, because I am writing this in my later years and long since the events took place much earlier in my life, it's possible I am recounting what are distorted memories. Other relatives and friends— and there are still a few who were present at that time— might remember these things differently. Yet that's the nature of recalling the historical. History relies heavily on who's telling it and writing it, and of course when they tell it. What is presented here is this writer's reality.

I also feel a need to write this remembrance because our remaining family, especially our sons, Frank, Edward and Matthew, and our two grandchildren know virtually nothing about their grandparents' lives and even less about their great-grandparents. Although my father had died before any of them were born, my mother was alive well into our sons' twenties, I hope they have fond memories of her spending time with them, taking them places, especially to beaches, talking with them, sometimes praising or reprimanding them, and being in their lives. But they have little history about their grandparents' earlier lives, even their names or any information about their long journey from their origins.

With this account, I hope to strengthen their connections to their long-dead relatives. Though I have few written records documenting my parents' lives, this memoir lets me share my memories with them. I hope my children and grandchildren will share this, perhaps add to it by writing about their own recollections down the road. If so, the journey will never end, and somehow there is a beauty to this.

It is worth noting that several years after my father died my mother remarried a rather traditional Italian-American widower, Andrew Trentin, who died at least several years before my mother. This memoir focuses exclusively on Frank and Philomena and their children, Maria Dolores Muzio Russell and me, Joseph Nicholas Muzio.

CHAPTER II

THE JOURNEY BEGINS

M Y parents' tales, their journeys, cry out to be told. Phyllis Brancata and Frank Muzio were significant and vital, as so many other parents. And like so many others, they were struggling, persevering, loving, resourceful, enduring and in many ways complex, even unknowable or unspoken in certain ways. Both were intelligent, and they were supportive of my sister and me. And every day they made significant contributions to the lives of many others on their way.

My mission in this project is to tell about their voyages, forthrightly, and with unabashed honesty. Also, since I am now well into my mid 70s, I want to be sure this mission is fulfilled while I am still healthy and fully cogent, or at least that's what I believe. When I thought about starting this personal writing project so long ago, I thought it would be a simple and straightforward task that I could complete in perhaps a dozen pages or so. As it turned out it has been none of these and after several years it is done, at least I think so. As a writer, it is difficult to know when something is finished, the way you want it to be.

In addition to believing that my parents' life histories deserve telling, I have another, more private, even selfish motive, that this detailed exploration into the past might help me reach a clearer understanding of myself. Who am I? How did I become the person I am? What took place to bring me to this point in my remaining days?

Much of whatever I have become is the direct intrinsic result of my parents' continuing influence on my life. They wove their Italian-American and Roman Catholic backgrounds and values into the fabric of their childrearing beliefs and practices. They transmitted to us their values—loyalty, family commitments, behaving honestly and ethically, excelling in school, fighting for causes, not letting people hurt or abuse you, a belief in hard work—along with many other traits, including some I might be unaware. Some of my family and dear friends might question some of these parental forces. But my life is forever entwined with theirs.

The lives of Phyllis Brancata and Frank Muzio do not especially warrant any scholarly analysis; nor is it likely anyone else will write their stories. But I am doing this because I am their son. There are certain, clear realities. My parents did not change or help resolve any major societal problems; they seldom joined groups or fought for broader causes. They did not play critical roles in their communities. Nor did they make any type of discoveries, or invent or create anything, and neither of them acquired great wealth, power or influence. Their career efforts were not particularly successful. On the other hand, neither of them had any drug, alcohol or legal problems, or any other kind of notoriety. My father, as I will describe later, intentionally avoided calling attention to his life. Overall, some may see their accomplishments, their very presence as uneventful or insignificant, similar to many others. Even some of those who read this account may agree. It doesn't matter. They were here and had worth. No, more than that.

They lived out their lives primarily in twentieth century urban New York City environs. They worked hard most of their lives with purpose and dignity, and did not complain about their lives, or their unfulfilled dreams and hopes. They were part of that endless energy flow of humanity, forever linked to the billions born before them and since. They came here, lived and died. At some point, their remaining family and friends will forget them, and they too will die.

Most of the written records of their lives are already lost except for a few remaining hospital documents and death certificates. Sometimes what is available was transmitted orally. All of this translates into having less reliable information than we want. I did not devote much time to seeking out possible records of their lives. (My editor and his colleague did provide new information to me about their journeys to America available via computer sources.)

There is no indication that either of them came from anything but poor peasant southern Italian stock. My father came from Calabria, near the sole and arch of Italy's geographic boot, my mother from slightly further north, but still in southern Italy. Neither of them seemed to be clear about their ancestors in Italy. Like millions of other immigrants, Philomena and Frank came as unknowing children with their parents to the United States to find a better life, work hard and raise a family. It is their ancestry coupled with the lives they lived in America that made this family what it is today.

I will tell the tales of Philomena Brancata Muzio and Frank Muzio in separate chapters, first writing about my mother and then my father. It shouldn't surprise anyone that the events of their lives overlap. After all, they grew up in the same downtown Manhattan neighborhood, knew of one another for years before they married, and they were married almost 30 years.

For the most part, like any marriage, theirs seemed to work fairly well most of the time. They were affectionately demonstrative to one another and in the privacy of our home there were frequent signs of a comfortable love relationship between them. When we traveled as a family, I recall my parents holding hands as they walked with my sister Maria or me. They kissed each other when parting or coming together. My father enjoyed hugging my mother, and she would smile when this happened. There was a great deal of kissing and hugging between the children and our parents. Even when we were adults, we kissed our parents. (This still takes place now between our children and us.) When we went to the beach or parks, or lots of other public places, they kept a close eye on their children without smothering their freedom to reasonably explore independently. When they were with others, my parents joked with one another and the others, but rarely criticized each other. Of course when they got home and were alone, their discussions could be more personal and direct. They got along day to day, carried out chores cooperatively, and had the capacity to leave certain matters temporarily unresolved without any public reprimands.

But, they also had occasional disagreements. Sometimes they argued in a reasonable way. At other times both could be deeply upset and angry, especially when the discussions became heated. Then, for a while, they wouldn't talk directly with one another, and would use my sister Maria or me to convey their words back and forth. We were verbally integrated into their ongoing dialogue. This seemed peculiar because we were all in the same room and they could easily see and hear the other. Even as children it seemed silly to us, but we complied. In a day or so this would be over and matters would be calm until the next time.

Though they were both completely Americanized and fluent in English, they sometimes reverted to Italian to keep my sister and me from understanding. However, their tones and decibel levels gave us the idea. They also spoke Italian when they were talking about something they preferred be kept away from their children, a piece of gossip or some other familial revelation. These topics were not to be shared with their offspring. Interestingly, they did not encourage their children to learn or study Italian. If they had, we would have understood what they were talking about. They definitely didn't want this, especially when we were young.

Throughout their marriage, my parents took diametrically opposite approaches to money matters. My mother was forever frugal, and extraordinarily cautious about spending. She believed in methodical saving and hesitated to do anything that could be a waste or considered a luxury, apparently because of her upbringing. She worried about leaving the electric lights on in empty rooms; about food left on our plates; or wasting water. She believed it was essential to save some money each week no matter how little and in taking care of our belongings so we didn't have to replace them unnecessarily or foolishly. Any replacements had to be definitely needed and justified.

This caution often caused indecision along with heated discussions within our family. For example, my mother often wanted to look at homes to buy. This became a ritual involving all of us. As a family, we spent many Sundays over

many years with real estate brokers in Queens, particularly
Butterly and Green, on Hillside Avenue in Jamaica. As young
children, we didn't like doing this and tried to get out of it,
but we had to go along anyway. She thought it would be good
to buy a home in Forest Hills Gardens or Jamaica Estates,
two of the more prestigious and attractive residential areas
in Queens. We even occasionally traveled further out on
Long Island to different communities. But it never happened,
either because she couldn't decide, my parents couldn't agree
on the house or she just didn't follow through because she
came to some realization such a venture would consume
money. Later she'd regret not having done anything and
would let us all know about her disappointment, especially
after the value of those houses she'd looked at continued
to rise. She had a long memory about these unrealized
purchases and expressed her regrets.

She acted similarly when buying stocks, rather, not
buying them and then forever regretting it. Even when she
didn't have much money and probably couldn't have invested
anyway, she kept talking about those lost opportunities.
Eventually, and after my father died she overcame her
hesitancy and eventually purchased and maintained a
considerable portfolio of blue-chip stocks. Her earlier
regrets about not buying those homes and stocks were
predictably after the real estate values and the stock prices
had consistently soared well beyond their original prices.
And they both soared for many years. Once the future was
known, it always proved she was right. But, when and if the
real estate and stock prices went in the opposite direction,
and sometimes they cyclically did, she would not mention
this downturn, nor would she focus on those supposed
missed opportunities when this did happen. Then, she had a

self-imposed amnesia and was non- communicative on these same matters.

By contrast, my father was a risk-taker, a high roller, someone who always seemed to find ways of making or gathering money, and also in spending it as if there was no tomorrow. He treated money as an adventure. He believed there was always more money out there and he was confident he could get it one way or another. He was impulsive about spending, always doing expensive things and buying expensive items, often without consulting my mother. He found places to play high stakes poker, and on Sundays knew where to find the high-betting dice games in Brooklyn and Queens. He loved to roll the dice and to bet, and he looked for action. He was much more relaxed about taking chances and doing things than my mother, making plans to travel, going out for dinner, and other ways to loosely spend money. They had similar childhood backgrounds, but remarkably different responses and attitudes about money and its uses. Of course, their beliefs and behaviors, like all of ours, were the result of those imperceptible childhood forces and circumstances that shaped their personalities and their approaches to life. We'll never know a full answer on this.

For many reasons, we know much more about my mother's early years than we know about my father's. My mother was able to spend more time with her large family, sharing experiences for a much longer time. However, my father was out on the streets of Manhattan from about age 12, spending far less time with his family, so we have fewer details. His sisters married early, moved away and were gone. We do know that my father lost his father, Nicholas, and his older brother Joseph at relatively early ages. In addition when he was an adult, he had a long time, severe falling out with one of his sisters, Tessie. (More about that later.) My father never told us much about his parents or his early years; maybe he had fewer memories because he was on the streets so young. Or perhaps he was hiding something he didn't want to reveal. As a result, some of the details about my parents in this memoir came from others, usually close relatives who were with them at the time.

CHAPTER III

PHILOMENA'S JOURNEY

M Y mother Philomena (note, not yet Phyllis until much later) Brancata was born January 21, 1903 in Fernandina, a small village in southern Italy. I recently received information that Philomena arrived in New York in 1906 along with her mother, her older brother Domenico and her older sister Elisabetta to meet her father, Egidio in Manhattan. She became an American citizen January 10, 1928 in the U.S. District Court of the United States in Brooklyn, an event recorded in Naturalization Certificate #2513198, Petition Volume 288, and number 82547. Philomena married Frank Muzio in Manhattan in September 1928. She died at 82 on May 29, 1985 in Queens. My father Frank was born on February 28, 1891 and died April 27, 1958.

Phyllis and Frank's daughter, Maria Dolores Muzio, was born January 29, 1930 in Brooklyn. Maria died May 22, 2000. As the birth and death dates of these three Muzios are brought together, there is a seeming connection I have established. All three were born in the winter, and all three died in the spring. Once in a while when springtime becomes a hint and rolls around, I think about how both my parents and sister died in April and May, and wonder if it will be the same for me.

Phyllis and Frank's only son, Joseph Nicholas was born on June 4, 1932, at the Bay Ridge Sanitarium, in Brooklyn. A sanitarium simply means a clean or sanitary place, where they focus on preventing illness. When I was a child and was told about being born in such a place, somehow it was unclear what this meant. Fortunately, I am still around and able to write this Brancata/Muzio family saga.

The year 1903, when Philomena Brancata was born was the same year the Wright Brothers first flew, getting their plane off of the ground several times for distances varying between 120 feet to the longest flight a distance of 862 feet. When I was young and found my mother was born that same year, I made a peculiar, continuing mental connection between her and the Wright Brothers.

Strangely, we were never sure whether her birthday was January 21, 22 or 23. There was no single, consistent birth certificate available to verify the actual date. She told us she was born in Fernandina. Official records of more than 100 years ago were typically kept in the small town halls and in churches, and those buildings and others were subject to earthquakes, floods, fires and even wars. So for a while we celebrated her birthday on any one of those three dates. Eventually, to reduce any further confusion, we settled on January 21st. It was comical when we first found out even she didn't know the date. She always said it didn't really matter; the dates were close enough together. That was typical for my mother; she never made a big deal out of a seemingly insignificant matter if it suited her thinking at the time.

In addition to the confusion about Philomena's birth date, we were never sure about the definitive spelling of her last name. How could that be? Doesn't everybody know how to spell his or her name? Not really, it depends. It might have been Brancati, Brancata, or Brancato, or perhaps another similar name. We discussed this topic over the years, but we never fully resolved it. Thanks to my editor Richard A. Danca, he located the ship's manifest of the SS Europa, and my mother is listed as "Philomena Brancata." Usually, perhaps out of habit or some unspoken agreement, Brancata became the preferred spelling for my mother, and her siblings and their children.

In May 2007 Lois and I were traveling in southern Italy. Before we left I had intended to go to some municipal building in Fernandina or Bari look for her birth certificate and the recorded birth name. However, once in Italy I chose not to do it. It didn't seem to matter that much. I came to believe I would never find the information I was seeking. Besides, we were traveling with our dear friends Rose and Michael Mahoney. With all of the beauty of Italy around us, along with our busy itinerary, I chose not to involve them in my personal quest. Perhaps there will be another time.

Philomena was the child of Maria Tucci and Egidio Brancata. We do not know what occupations her parents had in Italy, but we confidently assume they came from peasant stock. Before coming to the United States, her father went to Rio de Janeiro, where he spent 2-½ years working as a street cleaner. We do not know when he did this. He was there without his family, saving his earnings, which must have been meager, so he could return to Italy and bring his family to the United States. Who can explain why someone would leave his family, go to South America alone, work as a poorly paid street cleaner for years or how it was possible to save enough money so he could gather up his brood back in Italy and bring them to this country? What possible forces could have driven him? In addition to Philomena, this brood included an older sister, Elizabeth (Elisabetta), an older brother Dominick (Domenico), and two younger sisters, Lucille and Rose, both born in Manhattan. Rose, the youngest, is 97, lives in an assisted living facility in Ogdensburg, New York, near her daughter Francine. The others are long dead.

There had been another son, Daniel, but he died of pneumonia at eleven months. We know little about him. He's buried in the family plot at Calvary Cemetery in Queens, along with other family members. After Daniel's death, Philomena's mother traveled with a neighbor from lower Manhattan to Queens on the subway to regularly visit Daniel's grave. She would leave candy on the headstone or at her dead baby's plot. Interestingly, Jews and Hawaiians, and maybe others, leave stones or flowers as a sign of remembrance and concern. But I had never heard of leaving candy for the dead. My mother never told us what her mother thought would happen to this candy, and no one questioned her motives. Even so, she must have done it because her mind and her religious beliefs told her she was expressing love and attention for her shortly lived dead child. Candy is so reassuring to a child and to the adults giving it out, too.

There is some confusion as to when Philomena came to the United States from Italy. My mother told us she came here twice, once when she was three in 1906 and then a second time in 1909 when she was six. We know nothing about the sequence and details of these two journeys, why there was a return trip to Italy at so early an age. It isn't surprising that Philomena spoke no English when she arrived; neither did her parents nor the older children in her family, all born in Italy. However, young children have the ability to acquire additional languages quickly, and so it was with her. There is no evidence her parents ever became fluent or could even communicate in English at all. Most of their neighbors spoke Italian or other European languages other than English. Her parents stayed with their Italian, but the children made significant linguistic progress, thanks to the neighborhood and the New York City schools. Gradually, she became bilingual, and eventually used English almost exclusively. In short, she'd essentially given up her native language as a young child.

Over the years, especially as an adult, when she wanted to communicate in Italian Philomena spoke a dialect that somehow blended into it a New York accent, and this often led to confusion about some of the words and phrases. So there were times when people speaking more fluent, classic Italian didn't understand everything she'd said. Nor did she always understand them. This happened when she visited Italy as an adult and would try to speak her New York dialect Italian. Italians didn't understand her and she didn't understand them. Yet people recognized her sincere efforts and were polite as they picked up each other's phrases. Later on, in various workplaces when she'd try to better understand Italians there was similar confusion, but she was able to assist them.

The Brancata family settled first at 21 New Beaver Street in Manhattan, then on Franklin Street for a brief period, and later moved more permanently to 72 Baxter Street in lower Manhattan, where their lives in the United States had rather humble beginnings. Though the word "humble" might imply some less harsh or painful conditions, their lives were essentially unpredictable, consistently difficult, sometimes overwhelming, and eventually tragic.

Philomena's mother was the superintendent of the Baxter Street building, a five-story tenement crowded with other large, "humble" immigrant families. The super's children, especially the older ones, performed many of the superintendent's maintenance duties for the building. Some of these were arduous assignments, which had to be done regularly and properly. Rose, the baby of the family, did the least and was frequently exempt from chores. Rose said that she was treated in special ways, maybe even spoiled, especially by her father; she seemed to be his favorite and recalls being given pennies to go to the local shop for sweets.

Philomena had a totally different experience. She frequently told us that she and her younger sister Lucille had to scrub five stories-worth of marble/tile floors and stairs and clean the building's brass handrails every Saturday night, usually later at night. Then early every Sunday morning the building's owner came by to check their work, scrutinizing what they'd done as thoroughly and compulsively as any United States Marine Corps Drill Instructor would inspect his platoon of recruits before granting liberty. If he wasn't satisfied, the children had to change out of their clean church clothes and redo the unsatisfactory jobs. Only when he was completely satisfied could the family now go to mass at the Transfiguration Church on Mott Street, often having to go to a later mass as a result. Just like the Marine Corps, there were no excuses for their supposed or real poor performance. Corrections had to be made.

I once asked my mother why she and aunt Lucille had to work so late on Saturday nights. I thought it might have been because it reduced the chance someone dirtying the floors before the next day's morning inspection. She told me that was part of the reason, but there was another one. Her mother wanted this. Typically, the men who lived in the building were back in their apartments by 9:30 p.m. This made it safe for the young girls to do their chores without the men looking up their dresses at their legs and underwear while they were kneeling and scrubbing the hallways and steps. I never understood how she or her mother knew that all the men would be in their apartments by then. Didn't any of them stay out later?

It's hard to believe my grandmother would worry so much about this. At the time my mother was only 8 or 9 and her sister Lucille was 6 or so. Their clothing was layered and lengthy and undoubtedly could reveal nothing, except in the mind of their mother. You'd need X-ray vision or would have to stand directly underneath them, or perhaps turn them upside down to see anything. Nobody seemed to question the absurdity of this argument, as well as the visual impossibility of looking up the garments of totally covered young children. Besides, who other than some potential pedophile would even want to look? But mother had spoken and the children complied. That was the way things went. Grumbling, questioning or non-compliance were not options.

Philomena's mother, Maria Tucci, was one, serious, active, resourceful businesswoman, driven to keeping the family in line with her values from Italy. Making money was important, a continual need and activity. There were many mouths to feed in the Brancata family. One source of income among several was selling Javelle water to her neighbors. Many immigrant families used this then-popular bleach for washing their clothes. Javelle water was still available from street venders in Brooklyn well into the early 1950s. I

19

remember smelling Javelle water as a child; it reminded me of the strong bleach odor in public swimming pools.

She also sold olive oil to neighbors, adding a few pennies to the price per gallon she had paid, and she did the same add-on with cheeses. In addition, she allegedly loaned money to others, charging lower interest than the banks. No one knows where this extra money came from, how she got it or how this unspecified lending system operated. There are no records, and the few remaining relatives from that era recall little about this venture. She allowed a local bookmaker to install a phone in her apartment, for which she received a weekly fee. But the family couldn't use this phone, and didn't have one of its own. No one asked questions about this venture, or at least that's what I was told.

My mother's father Egidio was a diminutive man but a hard worker. He held two jobs. One was some sort of low-level clerk's position in a business office downtown; no one knows or talks about the other full-time job. Because he usually worked six days a week for about 16 or 17 hours each day he wasn't around the rest of family much. Even when he was around he had little to say. His children (my aunts) later said he was a quiet, gentle father. Today we might try to provide a clearer psychological explanation for his silence and distance beyond his arduous work schedules and to consider the possibility he was depressed and overwhelmed with life itself. Family members rarely spoke about him, perhaps because of the abrupt circumstances surrounding his death, which I describe below.

Italian families tend to be matriarchal. Italian males believe and present they are fully in charge of the family and they want the world to know it. But the real familial power lies with the women. The men may talk, even brag to their buddies in coffee shops and on street corners, but the women make the critical major decisions. This was certainly true with my mother's parents. Her father worked diligently, silently, and was absorbed in those two jobs he had. The power and control for the family rested primarily with her mother who ran this family and its finances from the tenement on Baxter Street.

In Manhattan in the early 1900s, and probably in other cities, there were few organized support systems for immigrants once they arrived and took up residence in those unsanitary and overcrowded tenement buildings. In these humble beginnings (again, note the use of the term humble) they relied mostly on other families and friends, or just themselves. This informal support system promoted a sense of involved community membership. Once you were here, you eventually helped those after you if you had any sense of kindness, decency and commitment, remembering how you'd been helped. But not everyone helped or lived by these loosely established protocols; some behaved selfishly and forgot their roots. Some immigrants were exploited and were victims of crime, including those within their own networks. As in any system, some were just takers, abusers and exploiters.

Some immigrant families eventually moved away to better locations, sometimes as far away as Brooklyn, Queens, even Staten Island, only a ferry ride from where they had been living downtown. Most however, assisted, bartered or donated and were the recipients of other people's generosity and good will. And if none was available for whatever reason, then, like so many others, you struggled, did without, found ways of getting something done, sometimes even stole. You eventually recognized that life in this country was not as pleasant or beneficial and didn't meet your high and unrealistic expectations. You were here and found ways to get by.

For the most part, immigrants worried about meeting those basic daily needs, especially "putting bread on the table" and finding a modicum of basic comforts and occasional rest. Many immigrants never expected that life in the United States would be so difficult or harsh. Too many of them had been deluded by rumors that the United States was the land of milk, honey and gold and they found survival difficult. Some found it so overwhelming, they gave up chasing the dream and returned to Italy with their disappointments.

Most immigrants preferred to believe that this truly was a land of total opportunity. Such myths persisted even when they faced the reality of living, working and walking on those streets. Yet, for the bulk of them, the reality of America was still better than the poverty, deprivation and harsh conditions in their homeland.

Although I've mentioned that immigrants had few outside resources to help them, the Brancata family, and others on and around Baxter Street, did get some assistance from the Children's Aid Society and the local Roman Catholic Church of the Transfiguration on Mott Street, which is still there. Early on they provided clothing, English lessons, food, religious instruction and spiritual comfort. Philomena always remembered the help and support of these two groups. For the rest of her life, she regularly contributed to the Children's Aid Society. Later on, she encouraged her children to do the same and we did. Today's Children's Aid Society is still a major institution in New York City, providing many diverse and wide-ranging supportive and educational programs.

Philomena never finished high school, apparently leaving after only a year, possibly two, a common, even expected occurrence. Immigrant parents didn't encourage girls to continue in school, believing that they would be better off getting an office or factory job, finding someone to marry, having babies right away and raising a family within their tight-knit neighborhoods. *La Famiglia* was paramount. Being a high school graduate back then was probably the equivalent of successfully completing college these days. Perhaps even more in some respects. Many high school programs were rigorous and good preparation for taking a job. But, with mouths to feed and the younger family members not working, and more babies usually on the way, a job and pay took priority over attending school. Later the other children found jobs, part-time or even full-time. My mother probably learned to take shorthand and to type while still in school; these skills along with her pleasant appearance and cooperative attitude helped her find office work.

Later in life and after much nervousness and intense study, my mother did achieve a General Equivalency Diploma or GED instead of a high school diploma. I recall her sitting in our living room when my sister and I were young and laboring over the preparatory books. This was difficult for her, and my mother did not react well to stressful situations thrust upon her, but she did it. I could always tell when she was stressed. She would become agitated, her voice would be sharper and she would move about in a hurried manner. Sometimes, she would inexplicably busy herself with some inconsequential or meaningless chore just to avoid the seemingly difficult task, but her stress responses still showed.

Sometime just after World War I, when she was 16 or 17, my mother was thrown into a highly disconcerting and stressful situation. While at work as an office clerk or typist in a Wall Street firm, she was suddenly told to go home right away; there'd been some sort of accident. No one told her what had happened, only that she'd find out more when she got home. She rushed home and found a neighborhood crowd and the police outside her building. She immediately learned that her mother had died in an accidental fall from her fifth-floor apartment. She had been trying to hang wet clothes on a clothesline outside the window but the lines and pulleys were frozen, covered with ice. To get on with her chores, her mother had tried to loosen the frozen line by pushing and pulling back and forth. When the frozen line abruptly yielded and gave way, the force and momentum of her last vigorous push on the line thrust her out the window. She landed in the yard on the hard frozen earth five stories below. She was dead.

My mother had had difficult experiences with her mother; her mother constantly made demands on her, and frequently hit her if she'd behaved in an unacceptable way, or her mother thought she had. Even so, she loved her mother, understood her personal struggles and was deeply affected by her sudden, tragic death.

Eight days later, while the family was still mourning the unexpected loss of their matriarch, there was another unexpected tragedy. Again while she was at work, my mother was told to go home. Again, as she arrived, the neighbors were gathered on the street, and again there were police cars. Inside the house, she found her father had hanged himself in the cellar. She and others, including two of the police officers went into the basement and cut him down. We never understood how or why she got so directly involved in this terribly upsetting task. Nor do we know a fragment of why her father killed himself—as if there was ever a reasonable explanation to selfishly disengage with such finality from one's family and to yield precious life itself. Apparently, this sudden unexpected burden of becoming a single parent just 8 days ago combined with the sadness and depression of his life was too overwhelming for him. His wife had been the controller and principal, and he couldn't handle the burdens, hers, his, the children's. He was totally on his own. We are not all strong and competent, some of us waiver precipitously and relinquish to the pressures. They choose death over life. There is no definitive answer or rational explanation for such behavior. What is going on in the person's mind as life itself is forever yielded?

Within a week or so, this immigrant family of three young, unmarried daughters and one son was cut away from their parents, their presence and influence lost, along with their vital patterns and earning capacities. The fifth child and oldest, Elizabeth, was already married, with at least one or two children and probably pregnant with another. Shortly afterward, the remaining Brancata offspring, Philomena, Lucille, Rose, and Dominick, left the now parentless apartment on Baxter Street and moved to Brooklyn. For a while they would live with their sister Elizabeth and her husband Joe Stramiello along with their own expanding family. Dominick married shortly thereafter, leaving the four sisters together as when they were young. That didn't last long.

This tragic sequence of suddenly losing both parents so early in her life and being with them right after each died so unexpectedly imprinted my mother for the rest of her days. She seemed to be forever controlled by their abrupt losses when she was a teenager. At times she was quiet, self-contained and seemed to be elsewhere, preoccupied with her thoughts. It wasn't as if she was involved in some creative or busy activity taking up her time and energy, she just seemed more pensive and distant within herself. Most of the time, she was pleasant, loving, attentive and spirited. I can remember her occasionally talking about those events, full of the descriptive details, passion and tears, and ending up pacing and sobbing. It was as if it was an unfolding of a sad, heavy, morose play, its dimensions made it seem to be a fantasy tale. The last time I heard my mother's tragic tale was when Lois and I were living in Leonia, New Jersey a long time. Then it might have been a few years before she died. Each time it was as if a unique and fresh version of a passion play was being performed a few feet away. There was much sorrow. And each time she reminded me of the incredible Italian movie actress Anna Magnani, appearing somewhat tortured and perplexed in a sad film about post-World War II Italy.

Until one loses a parent or a child, particularly in the unique ways my mother lost her parents, no one knows how he or she'll react. There is no preparatory phase, no predictable sequence. There are always those who blithely tell us to "suck it up," or "get over it," or advise us to "move on." Others will advise the hurting person "time heals." Some even talk persuasively about "closure," whatever that means. These expressions may be fine advice in locker rooms or pep rallies, even to motivate someone at a sales meeting. But, they are merely just slogans, empty thoughtless words to supposedly promote resolution of something beyond resolution. There is no single prescriptive assuaging way to recover after such tragedy or loss. Maybe some never do. Perhaps silence is far more sensitive and empathetic. The silence conveys some secret dimensions. Words just get in the way, silence is clearer.

As she grew, my mother became more Americanized. She held on to only bare traces of her native language, and was pleased that she spoke and wrote perfect, flawless English with no hint she'd been born in Italy. Her efforts were so effective she never spoke in the stereotypical language pattern in which Italians supposedly added vowels to the ends of words or misused English terms. I am still offended by way television shows, movies, and some less-sensitive people who speak only English still mock and deride Italians, Jews, Blacks, Puerto Ricans, Poles, and others whose first language wasn't English. They artificially create superiority.

My mother often discussed these offensive jokes and remarks about Italian-Americans with my sister and me: The organ grinder with a dressed-up monkey, the shoemaker or barber who wasn't too bright and spoke peculiarly, and portrayal of Italians as perpetually in motion, arms frenetically flailing about as buffoons. She wanted to make sure we were aware of how unkind and damaging such remarks and ridiculous stereotypes might be to us. She didn't like jokes about Italians, or any other group either, and she would just stare at the teller of it. She didn't like derisions. She was slow to react to other jokes, too. Some thought she lacked a sense of humor. But she was disappointed that no one seemed to notice any more accurate and positive creative accomplishments of Italians and Italian-Americans in so many realms.

Philomena became a naturalized citizen shortly before her 25th birthday, and grew even more committed to her adopted country. She seldom talked much about her connections to the country where she was born. We don't know why she waited more than 20 years after coming to America to become a citizen; it was just some months shortly before she would marry Frank Muzio. However, she did speak frequently about the hardships that had motivated her parents to make the long, difficult journey to unknown America in steerage, the most harsh and crowded but least expensive accommodations on a ship. This is where the poorest people were packed below deck for the 10- to 14-day voyage to America. These poor, ignorant souls were prevented from any mingling with the passengers or even seeing or using the more comfortable and spacious facilities up above. For the rest of her life, Philomena remembered the crowding, the smells, the constant noises and especially disgusting mingling of humans with their wastes and vomit from seasickness.

In 1907 the famous photographer Edward Steichen took a photograph of immigrants on board a ship, it's titled "Steerage." A colleague and friend, Loretta Brancaccio Taras gave me a copy of it after I had told her about my mother's journey to America, and occasionally I still look at it. In the photograph, the faces of the immigrants are expressionless and seem to convey a distant loneliness and sadness to me. One black-and-white photograph can hardly capture those insensitive and deplorable conditions experienced by these immigrants.

Once here in America, despite the adversities they faced, the Brancata family never wanted to return to their impoverished peasant existence in Southern Italy. As mentioned, however, some did return temporarily a few years after being here. For them, America was an open, accepting country with all sorts of freedoms and unknowns. Many years later my mother did visit Italy again with her sisters to see her remaining relatives, and to look for the farm they'd lived on, which they still supposedly owned. No one knows what happened to this farm. My mother and her sisters had been told the Germans used it during World War II, abused it, and may have razed the buildings.

Philomena maintained an unspoken but rather loose connection to the Roman Catholic Church. Of course, she was brought up as a Catholic, exposed to all of the traditional childhood experiences of baptism, Sunday Mass, Holy Communion and Confirmation, and was probably married in the Catholic Church. She did marry Frank Muzio, who had been divorced so whether this took place in a Catholic Church is unclear. Maria and I only found out about our father's earlier divorce much later on. As a mother, she could be termed an absentee member of her local parish, seldom attending church services or other church functions. But she made sure both of her children were baptized, received their First Holy Communion and Confirmation, and that we regularly attended the religious instruction available to public school students after we no longer attended St. Ephrem's Catholic Elementary School in Brooklyn. Neither my mother nor father spent time speaking about their religious beliefs or insisting that their children believe in God. And they only went to Catholic weddings, baptisms and funerals of family members and close friends. At this point in my life, though, both my sister and I have long since fallen away from being practicing Catholics. I continued to believe and practice Catholicism well into the late 1950s before completely falling away. Maria fell away much sooner, she might have been shoved out the door, probably after leaving St. Ephrem's when our family moved to Sunnyside Queens.

Despite their irregular and unspoken commitments to Catholicism, no matter where we lived, my parents always had a crucifix directly over their bed. (Sometimes I had childhood difficulty distinguishing between a crucifix and a cross.) I remember theirs was a beautiful crucifix, a solid wooden cross, perhaps ten-to-twelve inches long and eight inches across the horizontal part, bearing a dull, metal replica of Christ, with visible nails through his hands and feet, a shroud partly covering him, and a prominent crown of thorns. Whenever they took the crucifix off the wall to paint or when we moved, the faint silhouette of the crucifix's position on wall could be visible until painted over.

Naturally, for many years I believed that this display of the crucifix might be evidence of my parents' overwhelming devotion to Christ and his suffering for all of us who were sinners. As I reflected over the years and my beliefs subsided, though, I decided it probably had some other less religious symbolism about their marriage and their lives together. We never discussed why the crucifix was there, it just was.

I remember picking up and examining the crucifix closely as a child. It seemed heavy in my small hands. The wood was solid and dark, and the dull-gold figure of Christ was dense but the lines on the head, body, and limbs, even the slightly protruding nails in his hands and feet, stood out. As a child developing a deep commitment to the Catholic Church, I worried whether holding the crucifix in these private, unauthorized viewings were some sort of sin but I never brought it to my parents' attention or told a priest in the confessional. It didn't seem too serious a violation.

Many times after my mother died, even recently in the past few years I have tried to locate this long-gone crucifix. It may have been misplaced or perhaps taken by some family member after she died in 1985. No one seems to know the answer and some are puzzled that I'm even interested after all these years. I had called my sister and Aunt Rose several times and they initially thought I was kidding around when I inquired about it. So did several called cousins. It took a while for them to know I was serious. It seems obvious to me that it's because the crucifix had long belonged to my parents, though perhaps there may be some other, unspoken reason. Even Lois has wondered about my quest for this religious symbol. At first she thought it might be some mysterious sign of my unannounced desire to return to the church. She knows I would never be so sacreligious as to hang it over our bed. Besides, our bed is up against a window, so, there'd be no place to hang it that way. Still, if any distant relative reading this happens to know where I can find my parents' long missing crucifix, I would appreciate it if they contact me. I might even offer a reward.

I even thought about replacing that lost crucifix. After seeing three wooden crucifixes in the front window of an antique store in New York one day, I went in and bought all three of them (it was cheaper to buy all three). Lois couldn't believe what I had done, since neither of us would have hung even one of them in our home. Sensing some concern from Lois, I later decided to give them to three more seriously committed Catholic friends. Each of them was pleased by the gift. So was I, knowing they would be displayed for serious intentions. Lois was both pleased and relieved, and knew one of them would not be above our bed.

No one knows why Philomena changed her name to the more Americanized name Phyllis. Perhaps it was an easier name to use at school or maybe she changed it when she started to work. It certainly made her identity seem less Italian or foreign. She was giving clear evidence of becoming more distant to her Italian roots.

Later on she took on an even more American name. My mother used to go to the movies a lot, even though she had limited funds. She particularly loved a well-known actress named Billie Burke, a flamboyant showgirl who was attractive, and had a high –pitched voice. My mother liked the name so much she adopted it, and then her friends all called her Billie. She used the name regularly, even signing everything but more formal documents with it. And, when Billie Burke shockingly bobbed her hair, so did Billie Brancata, Somehow, the name "Billie" seemed to fit her. It had a ring of casualness, warmth and familiarity, and it seemed to go with her broad smile and warm eyes. It was a safe, easy, comfortable way to address her, certainly more than Philomena or Phyllis. And it definitely sounded more American. Maybe this was just another effort to transform herself into a full-fledged American. She was Billie the American.

Based on early pictures I've found in family photo albums, both my parents were extremely attractive, well-formed and healthy looking. My mother was about 5 feet 2 inches, with classic Italian features, especially her straight, southern Italian nose, and her dark brown eyes and brown, soft, thin hair that never grayed. I always thought she was beautiful. For a person from southern Italy, she was fair-skinned, but she always developed a deep, rich tan, and her skin would glow. My father was no more than 5 feet 7 with a slender build, although earlier photos indicate he had been more muscular when young and also in the Army. He was bald at an early age. He too tanned well, but his natural skin color was darker than my mother's. He had prominent tattoos on both his forearms (more on this later). He dressed neatly and sharply. Many pictures show him in well-fitting jackets, contrasting slacks, crafted leather shoes and Panama straw hats.

When I was a teenager, I became aware of my mother's superstitious or "old world" beliefs. Some of these beliefs puzzled me, but since she was my mother I believed them, at least for a while, just as I first believed in Santa Claus or the tooth fairy. Still, it puzzled me that she could be modern in so many ways but paradoxically held on to some surprising (to me) almost foolish concepts. At about age 13 I began noticing changes in my body. There was new focus on my appearance and wondering if junior high school girls would perhaps talk to me instead of ignoring me. One day, while doing a thorough facial examination in our bathroom mirror and checking whether I had the beginnings of a pimple or two, I noticed a discrete, totally bald area on the left side of my head, just behind my temple. My hair had been cut quite short, almost shaved for some inexplicable physical commitment to older football athletes I'd seen and admired. I knew I was too young to be going bald but worriedly I showed it to my mother. She calmly said she'd known about it for a long time but never mentioned it. It was simply a birthmark, some sort of accident occurring before being born.

Her explanation fascinated me more. According to her, one day when she was pregnant with me, she saw a mouse running across the floor of the apartment my parents and my sister lived in Brooklyn. This frightened her and in her surprise, she yelled and jumped away, grabbing her bulging abdomen with both hands, pressing one of her fingers against my head while I was growing inside her. She believed that somehow this singular finger pressure on the side of my head caused my birthmark. Later on, I always asked barbers to leave this mark at least partially covered. As I got older and balder, though, it made no difference and this small area has blended in with the rest of the baldness.

My mother also believed that music and art were magically important to the child she was carrying. In those days music stores played music on speakers positioned outside the stores, hoping that the music would draw in potential customers. My mother deeply believed that this music would soothe and comfort the baby-inside her (no one called it a fetus!) and help it to properly develop, no matter what was playing. It might even endow the soon to be born offspring with talents in these artistic realms.

She felt the same way about visiting museums while she was pregnant. She believed that these great collections of civilization and human accomplishments would have a positive educational and cultural benefit for her developing baby. She never explained how the assimilation of these supposedly advantageous musical and cultural activities took place. I've never known if anyone ever tested such beliefs more scientifically, but that doesn't matter, my mother believed they helped, so they did. Maybe she was right. Certainly other identified in utero environmental conditions have been known to have bearing on pre-natal development.

My mother always dreaded fire. This inordinate fear had a strong, logical foundation in her life. When she was about nine months old, her older sister Elizabeth accidentally dropped her into an open fire while holding her as she was carrying out a chore near the flames. The family pulled the panicked, screaming baby away from the fire, examined her, and put butter or oil on the widely burned area of her head. In those days this treatment was considered helpful and healing. Now we realize that greases keep the heat intensely focused on the burn area and actually add to the damage site. As a result, my mother had a pronounced, easily noticed broad scar on the front temple side of her head. She always carefully positioned her hair to cover it, yet with her thin, fine hair, it was a lifetime cosmetic problem for her.

Ironically, although that incomprehensible, frightening, event as a baby stayed with her all her life, she didn't fear the small fire associated with lighting a cigarette, and she smoked for many years before giving it up. Thank goodness for that. If she'd continued as did her husband and daughter, she probably would not have lived as long and as well as she did. Unfortunately and pathetically, my father and sister never quit smoking and lung cancer and those related diseases shortened their lives considerably.

Over the years my mother was always innately afraid of lighting the gas stoves we had in our apartments and homes. She would ask one of her children or another adult if around to do this simple chore. When no one else was available, she would reluctantly bend down, strike the match, close her eyes and literally grope for the small gas opening. With her eyes closed, she rarely succeeded right away and it sometimes required a couple of matches. Meanwhile, of course, the gas kept flowing, filling the local area with a distinctive smell. She would often need a second match, sometimes a third; suddenly, there would be a minor explosive puff, mother would jump back, and finally the oven was lit and she could move on and do the cooking. Someone would open a window and the smell of gas would dissipate. This was a repeated pattern and was only modified with the advancement of automatic pilot lights on gas stoves.

Once when our family was having a big party at her apartment in Flushing, Queens, a fire broke out in the oven. This must have been about 1962, after my mother had married Andrew Trentin, when my son Frank was about three. My mother tried to put out the fire by herself without telling anyone else. When she failed, she quietly came into the other room, took her grandson Frank's hand and left the apartment. Meanwhile, within minutes, someone smelled something burning and we ran to the kitchen, where we saw the growing fire. Lois and Maria sprang into action, threw salt on the fire, hit it with some dishtowels and eventually were able to extinguish it.

Lois then ran through the crowded and noisy apartment in a panic looking for Frank, with no idea that his grandmother had already taken him away from the fire. We later found my mother and Frank in the lobby several floors down. My mother couldn't explain why she'd run out and said nothing to anyone. Clearly, no explanation could have expressed her dreaded fear of fire and her childhood experience. She reacted impulsively, able to protect only our son Frank and herself. It was pure self-survival.

Despite such events, she was easy to get along with, unlike my father who was usually gentle, but sometimes was explosive and disruptive. That doesn't mean my mother didn't get upset and angry over the years, but her episodes were infrequent, short-lived, and usually easily remedied. There were times when she was into her menopause, (about which as a teenager I knew nothing); she had some hot flashes and obvious sweating then, when she could be explosive and sometimes teary then.

My father was more mercurial. Everything could be cruising along when suddenly, without any announcement or obvious cause my father could explode with an overwhelming and disproportionate fury. Reacting to a particular situation or to words he found offensive, he could suddenly start yelling loudly, cursing and sometimes throwing things, fortunately in directions never hitting anyone. These incidents reminded me of how volcanoes can build up suppressed deep energy and then unpredictably burst and erupt spewing hot flowing lava all about.

Later, after a period of silence and solitude, he would apologize and seek forgiveness. But the outburst would unannounced, happen again, though not for a long while. Fortunately these incidents were rare and they happened less and less as he aged. Even at this point in my life I can recall several specific incidents, each with a frightening but fortunately temporary impact on the entire family. There were other explosive incidents outside our home, and I will discuss these later.

Maybe this is the time to mention my childhood nickname, Buddy. My father first called me this, and then the rest of our family joined in too. I'm pretty sure it came from his days in World War I when a soldier referred to another with this term of endearment and support. Some older family members still call me "Buddy," and sometimes so do I respond to this name, even referring to myself this way.

Perhaps because of those earlier sad experiences early in her life, my mother took on the role of some sort of social worker, except lacking a college degree, credentials, or any assigned caseload. She often helped people, even strangers, with food packages, new and used clothing, and money or unasked-for advice. Maybe this is why she was so involved with people when she worked as an intake/interview person for the Social Security Administration. She was created for such a position. She saw the downside and sad portions of other people's lives, never forgetting what she'd gone through in her younger years. She'd visit sick relatives and friends, send them get-well cards, she'd compassionately understand those who had had personal setbacks and urged us to understand their situations no matter how seemingly small.

When we lived in Sunnyside we used to send our laundry to the Brighton Laundry Company; the driver would pick up the dirty clothes, bringing them back the next week carefully packaged, clean and pressed. This was my mother's simple solution to never being able to put the correct amount of soap powder into the Bendix washing machine in our kitchen; she always added too much. Apparently she believed that more soap automatically meant cleaner clothes and invariably the kitchen was flooded with soapy water running from the machine. In any case, seeing the laundry driver every week made her worry about his finances. She gave him some of my father's used clothing; they were about the same size. The fact that the clothes were expensive and still wearable by my father didn't bother my father; it just gave him another excuse to replenish his extensive and continually expanding wardrobe.

My mother reminded my sister and me how important it was to help others, and she set the example in many ways. She often prepared bags of clothing or food for her brother Dominick and his large family in Brooklyn, which he had trouble supporting on his income as a barber. Sometimes she and her sisters would visit and help his wife Isabelle with washing, ironing and cleaning. Sometimes she'd ask Dominick to our apartment in Queens to cut my hair. She felt it gave him a way of helping us, even though barbers were right in our neighborhood. He didn't have a car, so he had to travel by train from Brooklyn. He'd bring the wooden stepladder from the kitchen into our bathroom, put a towel around my neck and start clipping. I remember him being a quiet man and he rarely said much during those haircuts, but that seemed OK to me. Once he'd finished, we'd clean up the cut hair from the floor, and he'd visit with my mother. She would give him some cash and, when he left, sent along the bags of clothes or food. Sadly and tragically, Eugene, his eldest son murdered him.

The clearest example of my mother's kindness and capacity to forgive involves the murder of her brother, my uncle Dominick. In about 1947, Cousin Eugene, the oldest of Dominick and Isabelle's nine or 10 children had a major dispute with his father. We don't know what this dispute was about, or for how long it had been brewing. But one day it exploded abruptly onto the street outside their house in the West End of Brooklyn. Eugene chased his father down the street and shot him with a handgun. His father died right there. Of course, newspapers like the Daily News and Daily Mirror carried the story. Both papers frequently reported the family tragedies in New York City. I remember being so thankful that none of my friends could connect me to the name Brancata that appeared in those articles. I never said anything about the murder, although I wanted to. I prayed that the story would die quickly and without any connection to my life or our own family's.

Eugene was convicted and sent to the penitentiary in upstate New York for 10 years. The case was not written up again in the papers, and I was relieved. My mother, while sad and deeply upset over the murder of her only brother, was still full of love and forgiveness. She periodically visited Eugene in prison and brought him some permissible items and a few dollars for his prison account. When Eugene was paroled after serving about seven years, my mother continued to offer to help him, even trying to get him a job. I have never understood how my mother could forgive the person who had killed her brother, but this was another pure manifestation of her intrinsic goodness. Once he was free, Eugene stayed out of trouble. He died of a heart attack a few years after his release from prison. We did not go to the funeral.

My mother's kindness continued throughout her life. While she was well and living in Holliswood, Queens, the man in the upstairs apartment, Mr. Pollack became less capable of taking care of himself. I think he'd been a Lieutenant or Captain in the New York City Police Department. Diligently, my mother took on more and more responsibilities, doing his food shopping, bringing him his mail, driving him places and staying in touch with Mr. Pollack's family. After Mr. Pollack died, my mother shockingly discovered that he had left her nearly $11,000 in his will. She never wanted it, never expected it, but of course, she accepted it, though she later told me it made her uncomfortable that she'd received the money instead of Mr. Pollack's relatives who believed they were far more entitled to it. At that point, their opinion didn't count.

One thing that did change over the years about my mother was her form. Although she had been slender when young, she had less success than she'd wanted in controlling her weight. But she still was attractive and looked years younger than her years. As she aged her body became sturdier and squarer: square shoulders, little indentation at the waist, pronounced hips and strong-looking legs that got heavier in her later years. When I asked her why so many of our family were short and stocky, she said it reflected our peasant roots, which she never forgot. "We're built close to the ground to make it easier for us to pick the crops." It seemed like a perfectly reasonable response, a logical connection between form and function. We used to call my mother "the Rock" for her stability and strength as much as for her solid appearance. Lately, when I stand in front of a full-length mirror I see how much I resemble my mother's build as she aged. I definitely share her body's square shape and the thickness of our thighs, as well as the lengths of our noses.

There were times I would get behind my aging mother and suddenly pick her off the ground and I became aware that she was heavier than I expected. She'd be surprised and immediately plead for me to put her down, but I'm not sure whether she was kidding, because she would be smiling. I always did, of course, and she'd smile and tell me never to do that again. But, of course I would, mostly when she least expected it.

In her adult years, my mother enthusiastically started many new activities but often gave them up a short while later. For example, she never learned to ride a bicycle as a child, so she tried later on. But she got frightened and stopped trying. She wanted to learn to play the piano and took lessons, but then found it too difficult. For a while, golf interested her. She bought a set of clubs, took lessons, practiced and tried it for a while. Then she quit and sold the clubs. Another time she took classes to help her earn her GED but gave them up, though she later passed the test anyway. The one activity she kept at throughout her life was swimming. She loved swimming far out from the shore at Rockaway Queens, in Martha's Vineyard when she visited us, in Maine while visiting friends, and of course in Florida. She also swam regularly indoors at the Flushing Queens YMCA on Northern Boulevard where she was a member for many years. When we were at beaches with her, she'd smile and tell

41

us how swimming made her feel good all over. She'd swim far out from shore and stay in the water a long time.

When Maria and I were younger and were on one of our winter trips to Florida for the horse racing season (our father was an authorized legal bookmaker at the racetracks; more on this later) our mother made sure we had plenty of opportunity for swimming lessons and water activities in the ocean or at the pools at the apartments where we stayed. She wanted her children to love swimming as much as she did. Sometimes our father would join us for fun in the water after he finished his work at the racetrack. By then, we had good lives, full of enjoyment and comfort, and we were secure children in a comfortable, stable, middle-class family. Maria and I were given many childhood privileges.

From the time my mother first worked as a teenager, almost all of her jobs were in offices. But she occasionally helped out in one of my father's restaurants. My mother hated the hurried, abrupt patterns of restaurant work, especially during the morning and afternoon rush hours, and she had a difficult time working with my father. When they did, they argued when they got home about how things should be done. My father was occasionally explosive when things went wrong in the restaurant and it hurt my mother to witness this or be subjected to it. She chose to work in a more orderly, quiet office environment, and because of her preferences, my parents got along much better when they weren't working together.

One office job she liked a great deal was working at Governor's Island, serving as a secretary to Anna Rosenberg, who was the head of the War Manpower Commission during World War II. In the early mornings and late afternoons, she'd be on the ferry between Governor's Island and downtown New York City. She loved the orderliness and remoteness of Governor's Island; it made her think she was off somewhere in the country, even though it was right in the middle of New York harbor. I recall how carefully she dressed in tailored suits, always with a hat and gloves. She never wore slacks to work because that would have been too informal and inappropriate during those years. Only on picnics or when she was playing golf or some other outdoor recreation did I see her wear comfortable slacks.

During World War II, when we were living in a third-floor apartment in Sunnyside Queens, my mother trained as an air raid warden after she tried to join the Women's Army Corps and was rejected. We never knew the reasons. Perhaps it was her age or the fact that she had two children and a federal government job. She took these air raid warden responsibilities seriously. She had to learn to distinguish between the shapes and silhouettes of enemy and friendly planes, just in case they flew overhead. She kept her brown army helmet, gasmask, armband, whistle and flashlight in a closet close to the front door, ready for action if warning sirens went off; and she attended required meetings to be up on the latest information and training about her patrols.

When there were air raid drills, she'd quickly grab her gear, run down the stairs (not safe to use the elevator) and rush to her assigned area on 42nd Street and 43rd Avenue. There she made sure all lights were off and all blackout curtains were properly in place. If not, she leaped into action, blowing her whistle, ordering people to close their curtains, turn out their lights, or do whatever else they were supposed to do. She was equally vigorous with any autos on the streets not properly dimming their headlights or failing to stop moving. We were at war, and like so many other millions of Americans, my mother took her volunteer assignment seriously. After all, the safety of our country and its citizens was at stake and she knew her responsibilities.

Even with her limited education, my mother was an avid reader and a fine writer. She always seemed to have a book with her, and she read to and from work, in the evenings, at just about every chance she could get. She spent a great deal of time corresponding with friends and family members, and frequently enclosed a small check for their children. She also kept diaries of her trips to other places. She belonged to the Book of the Month Club for many years, so there were always new books coming into our home. She read The New York Times in the morning on the bus and train to work. When I rode with her, I noticed she wore short gloves while reading so the newsprint wouldn't soil her hands. She also subscribed to many magazines, including Holiday Magazine, because she had a great urge to travel.

My mother extended her love of books to us. She always left books around for anyone to read and never tried to censor what we saw in books. And she encouraged us to read she thought were important. So, here were the Muzio children engrossed early on in reading James Jones' *From Here to Eternity*; Norman Mailer's *The Naked and The Dead*; Alan Paton's *Cry the Beloved Country*; Richard Wright's *Native Son*; John Gunther's *Death Be Not Proud*; John Hersey's *Hiroshima*, Laura Z. Hobson's *Gentlemen's Agreement*; and Irwin Shaw's *Young Lions*. Anyone who has read these books knows that some of them contain sexually explicit details. Others are sad and made us think about the world we were living in, or made us think about issues of bigotry, racism, human brutality and war. My mother often discussed these books with us. She made us strive to be clearer in our explanations and feelings, but without superimposing any of her opinions.

My mother also loved taking her children to Broadway plays and other events in the city. She also took us to museums, Rockefeller Center and parks in the city, and we'd usually stop for a meal or a snack on the way home. Because my father was often working, it usually was mother, Maria and me on these trips.

Luckily for us, my mother never gave up her incredible cooking skills. She prepared wonderful, large Italian meals, especially on Thursdays, Sundays and during the Easter and Christmas holidays. Some of these recipes became slightly Americanized by seasoning and the unavailability of some ingredients, but I never noticed a cookbook in our kitchen. She kept all her cooking secrets in her head. One of my regular assignments in the kitchen was to grate cheese. Sometimes I would eat chunks of the Romano grating cheese, enough to occasionally cause a small sore inside my mouth. But that didn't stop me the next time.

My mother was always demonstratively happy, pleased, when I brought home my friends, but Maria did this less often. It was as if we had a suddenly larger family. Childhood buddies Jerry Pagano, Larry Sullivan and Bob Wilson loved to visit our home, usually because they could always smell something good cooking and get a good meal. My mother believed in the concept of "feed me, love me." Whenever my buddies visited near dinnertime, she always fed them, even if they'd already eaten at home. After they finished the antipasto, pasta and Italian bread, they happily thought they were finished and fulfilled. But no, then came the roast beef or pork, plates of vegetables in olive oil and garlic, followed by bowls of fresh fruit. Unlike Jerry and me, Bob and Larry had never eaten so well. They came from Irish Catholic families where food was much more basic, perhaps less important. In visits to their homes I'd noticed they didn't spend a lot of time eating and talking, meals were quickly over. At his apartment, Larry Sullivan frequently had a pot of baked beans on the stove, or he would eat a cup of canned soup and some bread as his main meal, washed down by tea. That would never do in an Italian-American family; it would have been sacrilegious. This contrast made Larry a regular at our house; he was in a different culinary world.

I remember my mother making pizza dough and wrapping it in clean dishtowels, sitting it on the kitchen table or near the warm radiator to rise. If she briefly stepped out of the kitchen when she was slowly frying her outstanding meatballs in olive oil, I would quickly grab one or two and disappear. She'd always wonder how some meatballs had vanished but I'm sure she knew. Her tomato sauces were always superb, and for a while she joked about finding someone to market her secret recipe; she decided it should be called "Aunt Billie's." (Of course later on, some company began selling a jarred sauce it called "Aunt Millie's." I think it's still a major seller although there are many other competitive brands.) Because my mother worked full time, she'd prepare meals on weekends and we'd eat them throughout the next week. My father sometimes brought home meals from one of his restaurants, and he would do some serious cooking if he got home before she did.

When we were still living in Bay Ridge Brooklyn, my sister and I were friendly with the children of an Irish Catholic family upstairs, the Conklins. My sister once had spaghetti at the Conklins and came home bragging about Mrs. Conklin's wonderful sauce. My mother, who took exceptional pride, perhaps more than this, in her tomato sauce, was stunned and annoyed. After a few minutes, she called Mrs. Conklin and asked her what was in her excellent sauce, and how Maria had been so praising of it. According to my mother, Mrs. Conklin burst out laughing. She said: "Billie, I just open a can of Campbell's Tomato Soup, heat the concentrate and pour it on top of the cooked spaghetti." My mother was immensely relieved to learn that there was no way this Irish-Catholic canned sauce could possibly beat her carefully prepared, long-simmering Italian recipe, her Aunt Billie's special sauce which was based on years of tradition, probably passed on from her mother on Baxter Street.

When my sister Maria was older, she decided it was time to learn how to make our mother's sauce. I think she was aware that our mother was getting on in years. She watched carefully, even taking notes so she couldn't make a mistake or miss some unannounced ingredient. But when she diligently followed the recipe, our family taste testers decided that the sauce just wasn't the same, though it was close and quite tasty. Maria wasn't going to give up, that was one of her traits in so many other areas, she had my mother sit and write down exactly how she made the sauce, what the brands of the various ingredients were, and in what order to add them into the developing mix. But again, the sauce was still different. Finally Maria decided she needed to borrow my mother's old, well-seasoned cooking pots. They'd been in our family for so many years. Somehow that made no difference either. In the lifetime conflict between them, Maria was convinced that our mother had secretly withheld an ingredient or a procedure itself just to punish Maria and to prevent accurate duplication of her sauce. My mother always denied the accusation.

Maria's sauce was hers alone, and it was excellent, but it was never quite the same as my mother's.

No one is perfect, of course, but my mother never seemed to have any malice or foolishness about her and she was a wonderful mother in so many ways. Yet she had her peculiarities, too.

When I was an infant, my mother thought my ears stuck out too much from the sides of my head. My mother decided I should wear a soft cap covering my ears so they would stay close to my head as I grew. Where she got this idea was never revealed. Please don't laugh; although that's OK; she was doing what she thought best. By the way, my ears are plenty close to my head, but we do not have a test case to know if the cap helped. Later on in life she mentioned that her motives were to prevent them from ever sticking out the way the movie star Clark Gable's did.

She also thought I sucked on my fingers too much. Yes, I was breast-fed and perhaps I hadn't sucked long enough, but she was worried about my putting my fingers in my mouth long after being weaned. To solve what she thought was a problem with my finger sucking, she bought tiny metal cups and put them on my hands to hold my fingers together. She held them on with soft strings around my wrists. I have no idea what led her to that solution. One or two remaining and remembering relatives tell me now that, because I couldn't get to my fingers I would bang those damned cups on the high chair or on the struts of the crib. Again, please don't laugh; she thought she was doing the right thing. However, just imagine this poor baby with the cap on his head and his fingers tied into small metal cups. Someone seeing that today might have quickly considered calling child protective services, but back then that wasn't easily done. I have no idea if those metal cups succeeded, but I did bite my fingernails for many years as a child and even into early adulthood. I have read that nail biting is a form of aggression taken out on oneself. It took me a long time to give up nail biting.

My mother also believed in the supposed nutritional benefits of Jell-O. She thought it was good for our health, so she often prepared it as a snack or dessert. Too often. As a young child, I hated Jell-O, but she decided it was important for me. When I refused it, she'd force it into my mouth and keep my jaw tightly shut until the only alternative was gag on it and then reflexively and reluctantly swallow it. To this day I do not eat Jell-O. When I see it wiggling in a dish, I automatically gag and think back on that early childhood experience. When I mentioned this to my mother later on in life she said she never understood my resistance to Jell-O because it was so good for me. She denied ever holding my mouth totally shut, she was only encouraging me to eat it, and said I must have been exaggerating.

But at least I never got my mouth rinsed out with harsh soap as Maria did. One time when my sister and I were playing outside our apartment house without supervision, which was common in those days, an old Italian lady dressed totally in traditional black slowly walked by us. We knew she was Italian because of her dress, and I later found out she didn't speak English. To this day I do not know what possessed my sister to do this, but as the woman walked by, Maria spit towards her. Something about that woman bothered Maria. The woman found out who our mother was and went to her and in Italian told her what my sister had done. While my mother spoke Italian poorly, she still understood what the woman meant. Mother came outside, took Maria by the hand and asked her if the story was true.

Defiantly, Maria quickly responded that yes, she had spit at the woman.

With that confession on top of the old woman's descriptive announcement, our mother took Maria back into the apartment and into the kitchen where she grabbed a large bar of soap—bigger than Maria's mouth—and rubbed it onto Maria's lips and mouth. Maria screamed and our mother told her that was her punishment for spitting. Shortly afterwards, Maria's mouth swelled up, worrying my mother, who rinsed Maria's mouth with lots of water. Within a couple of days, Maria's lips returned to a more normal size and she did not seem to suffer much more. I remember that the soap was an uncolored bar marked "P & G," and that it was powerful enough to remove stains. I later found out it contained lye, a powerfully caustic ingredient. For a short period, my mother was worried, was sorry for what she had done and the whole thing was much out of character.

A few days later that same old Italian woman walked by Maria and me while we again played outside the apartment house. Maria stared at her, and spit towards her again, less directly than the first time. That was Maria's way of getting back and being even more defiant. She was her own person and even our mother's rough punishment wouldn't inhibit her. I think that the lady in black found a different route to walk, at least when my sister was outside. Maria remained feisty all her life, but without any blatant spitting. She became much more adroit using her mind and her words.

There's another story that shows a side of my mother we didn't like. When I was about 3 or 4 and Maria was 5 or 6, my father was a bookmaker at various East Coast racetracks (fully legal until states turned to pari-mutuel betting). Every year my parents left for Florida just after Christmas to find a place for us to live during the racing season there.

Sometimes my mother made the search by herself, though this often caused problems. Potential landlords sometimes cruelly told that they would not rent to her; they didn't rent to Jews. Door closed, and no further discussion. My mother was stunned and offended to be rejected because of her olive skin and the size of her nose. How's that for nasty stereotyping? She was angry for herself and for all the Jews. Sometimes she told the landlords she was Italian, but it didn't matter because they would not believe her.

Besides, she decided that she wouldn't want to rent from someone who hated anybody or any group and would tell the potential landlords that. She never had an unkind word to say about any nationality, religion, race, any group or individual. And she was not comfortable with any one who did, especially guests in her home. Still, my parents always found a place for us, usually a quite comfortable house or apartment. We stayed in Coral Gables, Palm Beach and other wonderful locations. We even had a nanny who took care of us and we attended nursery or play schools while in Florida. We had wonderful, joyful experiences in Florida each winter for a number of years. The living was easy, and life was good.

But, whenever my mother went on her search, she left us with our aunt Elizabeth in Bay Ridge Brooklyn for several weeks, and she lied to us, telling us she'd only be gone a short while and was only going to Abraham and Straus's, a well-known department store on Fulton Street in downtown Brooklyn. The trip to the department store normally would have taken about a half hour.

When she left us, and returned a week or so later, I felt abandoned, a feeling that's had a profound influence on me throughout my life, and I feel it even as I write this. Maria seemed less affected by it, or at least never mentioned it. I vaguely knew that we'd have to pay some kind of price for us to experience the beauty and benefits of going to Florida, but it upset me to learn that mother would tell us an outright blatant untruth, a lie. She did this whenever she went away, but I was too young to realize this, and I never knew her motives.

According to my aunts, after my mother left I would patiently wait a long time for her to return to my Aunt Elizabeth's house on 85th Street just off of 3rd Avenue in Bay Ridge. I would eventually stand or sit and cry at the front window for days, waiting and watching for my mother to return. My aunts told me I would stop crying and focus on something else, but I kept returning to the front windows to see if my mother or parents were coming back. Even as a child I understood that I had been waiting far longer than it would have taken my mother to return from any relatively brief shopping trip.

Why did my mother need to distort, to not tell us how long she or they would be away? Perhaps it eased her departure, but it was and still is painful to me. Maybe she only reflected the philosophy of the times that one didn't have to explain everything to children. Maybe it would be less traumatic if they didn't know the full story. Perhaps this was a leftover remnant of the belief that "children are to be seen and not heard" And that what we didn't know couldn't hurt us. Even today, whenever a close family member travels or I go on a trip, I feel certain forlornness and sadness, an inexplicable loneliness that gnaws at me until we arrive at our destination. I know my parents never meant to hurt me, to leave me feeling abandoned. And yet, I did, unsure of when they would return. I understand now that this was merely a temporary abandonment, they always returned; after all, some children are abandoned for years or forever, and that includes the death of the parent. But it still hurts.

Early in 1941 after my father opened a new restaurant in Long Island City, my parents moved from Bay Ridge to Sunnyside, Queens, mostly to make his commute easier. I was in the middle of my preparations for Confirmation at St. Ephrem's, and my mother decided it was best for me to complete them there. So, when my parents and Maria moved to Queens, I stayed behind, once again living at my Aunt Elizabeth's in Bay Ridge while I continued at St. Ephrem's. I was nine then, and a half dozen years beyond my earlier experiences of staying there when my parents went to Florida. I did what was told to do, and there was no discussion, no tears. Although my mother told me it was only for a few months, my earlier feelings of loneliness and disruption were there all over again. During this period, I took the train to Sunnyside on weekends by myself, staying with my parents and Maria, and then returned to Bay Ridge for the next week of school. The only thing I remember about my Confirmation was the Bishop gently slapping me on the face for some symbolic reason. After my Confirmation, and the end of the spring term, I moved permanently back with my real family.

Many years later, when my mother and I discussed these perceived desertions and my feelings of abandonment she told me she believed she was doing the "right" thing for me, that she never wanted to make us feel lonely. However, even though she knew that I was terribly upset and lonely when she took those trips to Florida, she had continued to pretend she was only going to Abraham and Straus'. How strange that in her attempts to prevent my loneliness she had unknowingly created it. The results of her misguided attempts are still with me.

I can still whip myself into what the author Joan Didion calls the "vortex of grief." I can climb right into that vortex as I re-live my mother's thoughtless and senseless unwillingness to level with Maria and me. Those childhood feelings of helplessness, abandonment and hurt remain with me today. Some people who may not know my experience tell me to "get over" these feelings. But that advice does not help me. How can anyone "get over" experiences that collectively seem so traumatic?

When any of our three sons has been separated from me for a while, such as taking long trips or going away to school, or even a vacation on their own, I have asked him (in what I hope is a calm manner), "Do you ever feel lonely or uncomfortable while you are away from home and your parents?" I've been asking this for years. But every time they give me a puzzled look and reply, "No, why are you asking me this?" I then drop the subject, and they let it go, too. Besides, why superimpose my feelings upon them? To this day I need to have regular communication with each of them even wherever they are. Perhaps now that they've read about this they will understand my incessant questions on this matter.

My mother also misled Maria and me when she decided completely on her own to get rid of our dogs, "Skippy" a beautiful Boston terrier, alert, reliable, and a dear friend, and later "Trixie" a Wire-Haired Fox Terrier. We got both dogs as innocent, vulnerable puppies and we too were innocent and vulnerable. For some reason, perhaps to avoid walking the dogs at night in inclement weather, or some of the related issues with having a dog, she eventually gave them away to someone, telling us falsely that they'd gotten lost, or hit by a car. Only much later in life, in a moment of confession, did she tell us what she had done.

Apparently she felt her actions would avoid hurting us, or prevent her from having to deal with our opposition to her goals. But her methods were terribly unfair because we were always hurt, especially me. I guess she just couldn't bear to tell us the truth, but we did suffer. Consider being told that your mother will be back shortly or that the dog you love was lost or worse, killed. While she may have meant well, and these decisions might have simplified her life it has been difficult for me to resolve my feelings of discomfort and uncertainty.

Later on, when we were teenagers, my father bought a fine, purebred boxer puppy, "Duchess." That dog was clearly, exclusively his, except when a reluctant teenage son in the family had to walk her. "Duchess" was almost always right near my father. She was powerful and constantly pulled on her choker chain. This dog was friendly, but remained untrained and undisciplined, often running out an open door and disappearing for a long time.

My father's remedy for this was to hit her on the nose when she returned or when she was returned to us, as if the punishment would ever encourage her to want to return on her own once she figured out what would happen. Although he'd read books on training dogs, they may not have had advice on dealing with a dog that ran away at every opportunity. Maybe he was using a technique he'd found successful when he was breaking horses in the army during World War I, but it certainly didn't work on this dog. My father had his own ways of doing things and it was unlikely he would have accepted any comment or advice. One day, in rebellion, the dog leaped right through the storm door of our house in Flushing Queens and just kept running. We never saw her again, though we looked all over. The glass on the broken storm door was replaced but "Duchess" had left us permanently. This escape was one rare dog disposal that didn't involve my mother.

In addition to her desire to enrich her children's lives with cultural things such as books, plays, and museums, my mother also wanted to expose us to other experiences that became available to lower middle class children in the 1930s and early 1940s. By today's standards, these choices were relatively meager. But, like many other things, they were better than nothing. In her efforts to quest for improvements for us, my mother decided to send Maria and me to summer camp, and also to have us take piano lessons. So, for two summers we went to a Mrs. Stuyver's Camp in Goshen New York. She also arranged for piano lessons with a teacher whom my mother in her inimitable kindness had befriended and for whom she felt sorry. The lessons allowed my mother to help this woman financially and at the same time enrich us musically. But we felt like sacrificial lambs.

We went away to camp those two summers, when Maria was 9 and 10 and I was 7 and 8. At the time, Goshen New York for this 7 or 8 year old might have well have been as far away as China, but I recently looked at a New York State map, it was only about 50 miles from Brooklyn. Except for the children of a physician in our apartment building, we were the only children in our neighborhood who went to camp at that age. I can't remember whether we went away for two weeks or a month, although either seems a long time for young children to be away. And yet it was mostly a positive experience for us. The counselors seemed to be young, friendly and interested in us. We played all sorts of games and sports and acquired skills; the boys against boys and the girls against girls and at about 10 o'clock each morning we had cold fruit juices. This was the first time I ever had cool pineapple juice, it was served in small paper cups and you could have more if you wanted. In the afternoons we rested. The boys and girls had separate bunkhouses. I only saw Maria at times when our recreational paths crossed. Everyone else was a stranger to me and I remember feeling uncomfortable, uncertain with them. Sometimes in my bunk at night, especially when we were first there, I could hear trucks on a nearby highway roaring along to someplace. For a while, I wondered if I could find my way to the highway in the dark, somehow stop one of those trucks and ask the driver to take me home to my parents. My feelings of loneliness usually subsided after the first few days. At the end of each camping session, the staff chose the best boy and girl campers, but we never knew how they decided. I was that boy in our first summer there, and still wonder why. Perhaps the award went to the quietest, least troublesome, most-compliant child, the one who caused the least difficulty for the other campers and the counselors. At that time, those criteria described me perfectly. As I became older and almost magically, those supposedly advantageous and rewarded traits at camp were lost forever.

The infamous piano lessons forced upon my sister and me are a less happy memory. At that time we were living in a lovely apartment on 73rd Street in Bay Ridge, Brooklyn. It was right near McKinley Park on Fort Hamilton Parkway and just a couple of blocks from St. Ephrem's Catholic School where Maria and I were students. The neighborhood was close to everything, including one of my father's restaurants, "The Red Apple" on Fort Hamilton Parkway. Somehow, my mother had become friendly with a middle-aged spinster who had had polio as a child, Philomena Adinudzio. Perhaps it was because they shared the same first name or maybe it was because the teacher's name ended in "zio" as ours did. Miss Adinudzio lived in an upstairs apartment near the Joseph Sessa Funeral Home on Fort Hamilton Parkway. Typically, my mother felt sorry for this woman's physical disabilities, her poverty and her rather shabby and unfortunate life. So my mother decided that more piano students would help her to survive. Unwillingly, Maria and I became the ones to serve this purpose.

I came to dread the lessons and never took them seriously or with any enthusiasm, and I ultimately found a way to get out of them. Miss Adinudzio was a short, obese, woman, with wildly flowing, curly hair. Watching her walk was an overwhelming sight. Because of her polio, she wore high-top laced boots and heavy full braces on her legs up to her thighs. She swayed awkwardly as she slowly walked toward me. To me, she looked like a monster.

Polio was a frightening and debilitating disease with no known cure, and it caused great fears across our country, especially for children. Much of the gear worn by those with polio was bulky and could do little to offset the afflicted physical limitations. In those years, President Franklin Delano Roosevelt had polio, though he'd contracted it as an adult. He hid his condition from the public even though he too required braces, canes and support from others. But I couldn't help notice Miss Adinudzio's grotesque (to me) appearance when I was in her dark, cramped, stagnant apartment.

Worse for me, Miss Adinudzio stank. After elevating her braced legs to fit under the piano with her heavy arms, when she sat next to me at her grand piano, leaning over the music pages, or reaching for my hands to show me the proper finger placement, I found her odor offensive. Sometimes I could see her hairy armpits. I found it extremely difficult to focus on the notes, finger placement and whatever she was telling me. She was an excellent piano player and might have been a competent teacher and looked so intense while she played, seemingly transported beyond her physical conditions and depressing apartment in Bay Ridge. But even after many piano lessons, I never got used to her odor.

My mother thought I was exaggerating when I complained about Miss Adinudzio's frightening appearance and odor. She felt I was uncaring and insensitive to the teacher's plight and insisted I overcome my dislikes and persevere. My mother had spent most of her childhood overcoming difficulties and she believed we should do the same. She was a strong believer in "gaining strength by overcoming adversity," either Emerson or Thoreau's statement. So the piano lessons continued even after we all moved to Sunnyside, Queens. Now I was 9 or 10 and I traveled alone on the subway to Bay Ridge for my lesson every Saturday morning. These days, such a solo journey might sound terribly unsafe, but it wasn't unusual then for children to use the subways and buses unattended, unharmed and unafraid. The trips gave me a chance to look around at the other passengers and also review my music books so I would be prepared for that week's lesson.

At some point, I simply stopped practicing. My ever-cunning sister Maria, in her efforts for me to survive Mrs. Adinudzio a little longer, helped me in my feigned preparations. Using a light pencil, she delicately lettered the ivory keys on our piano at home with the corresponding keys. She then wrote the notes in the music book. This trick worked fine except for two things. There were no marked letters on Miss Adinudzio's grand piano keyboard, and my sister had carefully erased the markings in the lesson book, so I was completely on my own. I was doing fine until Miss Adinudzio stopped me in the middle of the lesson to correct a mistake, and then told me to "pick it up" from a particular place close to the interruption. But I was only programmed to play the piece straight through, and my failure to comply upset Miss Adinudzio. I was a fraud, but there was no way I could tell Miss Adinudzio what I had done.

Though I knew I would never be a competent student, none of my pleading convinced my mother to let me quit Miss Adinudzio's music lessons. So I tried a different approach: I lied. I was still a deeply committed, practicing Catholic boy and knew this was wrong, but I rationalized it, knowing I could confess this sin to the priest the next time I made my confession. Once I got to Brooklyn, not far from my piano teacher's apartment, I would call my mother from a public phone on the street or in a candy store. I would tell her I was lost and had somehow taken the wrong train, ending up elsewhere in Brooklyn, maybe in far away Canarsie, which was like the country or some far away outpost to me. Of course she'd tell me how to correct my traveling error, but the trip would have made me late for my lesson, so she'd tell me to return home.

After doing this a couple times, I knew that my mother and Miss Adinudzio had figured out my deception. In an act of kindness and forgiveness my mother let me stop taking lessons. Perhaps I did confess my sin later on to a priest at St. Theresa's in Sunnyside. I never studied the piano again until I took some lessons from Bernie Shockett, a colleague at

Kingsborough Community College, thirty years later. Later, while we were living in Leonia, I took lessons from David Shapiro, another competent instructor.

Over the years, I came to believe that one of my mother's great strengths was her ability to empathize with other human beings. As I mentioned earlier, my mother was always helping someone, family and friends, people she met for the first time. We called her a self-appointed social worker without academic credentials or training. She took on this role intuitively.

Sometimes when working as an intake interviewer at the Social Security Administration she'd bring needy clients home, feed them, give them some clothing, even a few dollars before sending them on their way. My father would take her aside, out of earshot of our new guest, and quietly ask her why she was doing this. Her answer was always because they needed help, and no one was helping them. My father had no choice but to accept these newcomers to our home, he loved my mother and respected her goodness.

Remembering this reminds me of something that happened to me while we lived in Bay Ridge, Brooklyn, opposite McKinley Park on Fort Hamilton Parkway, something that upset my mother terribly and indicative of her reaction to certain situations. It was winter and a group of us were ice-skating in McKinley Park. Some children raced around the ice rink, sometimes slamming into one another, while others tried to improve their novice figure skating moves. Since it got dark early, my mother had told me to come home before dark; there were no lights at the rink and it was not safe to skate after dark. We were having such a fine time that I decided to disregard her instructions and stay with my buddies. As I was speeding around the ice in the dark, I tumbled right into the snow piled up on the side and opened a huge gash above my left eye. It bled a lot, the ice near me was dark stained with blood and I was scared, but hoped it was only a minor cut. It wasn't. Someone called an ambulance, which took me to a neighborhood hospital, where it took many stitches to close the deep gash. (In those days, I guess this could be done without any parental permission.).

When the ambulance dropped me off at home and a police officer took me up to our apartment, my mother screamed as soon as she saw us. My clothing was covered with blood, the area around my eye and temple was swollen, and thick bandages covered my eye. She held me close to her as she continued screaming, demanding to know why I had not followed her instructions. Then she asked, "How could you have done this to me?" It still amazes me that she could take it as subjectively as she did. It's as if I intentionally went out of my way to injure myself so I could intentionally hurt her. I guess I'll never understand that kind of logic.

My mother had a strong need to be with her sisters Elizabeth, Rose and Lucille, and sometimes visited with them several times a day whenever she wasn't working. She also stayed close to her brother Dominick, who always seemed more distant to me. Maybe that need for closeness was the unspoken residue of the tragedy of losing both their parents within eight days when they were all young. Or maybe it was because the sisters shared beds until they were teenagers, mostly because there was little space in their apartment. My mother always worried a lot about Dominick; perhaps she intuited that family's terrible tragedy.

The Brancata sisters were able to stay close because they often lived with or near one another, often shopping together, and always available to one another for any reason. An argument between a sister and her husband or between two of the sisters quickly spread through this tight network. It was not unusual for my father to help rectify the gambling problems of Lucille's husband Uncle Andrew, a decent and kind man whom I loved, and Elizabeth's husband Uncle Strike, a card shark who also had been a bookmaker and gambler. Uncle Strike, who later taught me all sorts of gambling card games, had known my father as a young man; they had been bookmakers and traveled together to bet on prizefights throughout the country. He was a tough, hardnosed person, but was gentle and funny with children. Elizabeth and Uncle Strike were married a long time and had five children, Marge (Kushner), Josephine (Strafaci), Marie (Ellis), Viola (Cuneo) and Eugene. Lucille and Andrew had two daughters, Andrea (Cataffo) and Stephanie (Boorman).

When my parents married in 1928, my mother brought with her into the marriage her two, beloved, still-single sisters, Lucille and Rose. It was sort of a package deal. At the time, Lucille was about 23 and Rose was 18, and they had depended on their older sister Phyllis since their parents' deaths. Apparently it wasn't "right" for them to have their own apartment, according to the mores of their culture back then. They lived with my mother, father, and later with Maria and me, but I do not recall how many years this went on. I do remember that they often called my father "daddy," just as Maria and I did. Perhaps they were trying to be respectful. Or perhaps our father had become their father, the one they'd lost long ago when they were so young.

There were many advantages to having my aunts live with us. Not only did they share chores and expenses, they were built-in sitters, giving my parents considerable freedom to go out to dances, parties, and the like. They regularly and willingly contributed to the rent and for food. Naturally, while they were sitting for us, they also had the luxury of having a date over without any supervision. In those days that was a rare privilege. This may seem archaic, perhaps inexplicable, by today's more liberated standards but those were the times and culture and that's the way things were done. Nobody seemed surprised by compliance to these ways.

Lucille and Rose were extremely generous to Maria and me while they lived with us and later on. They showered us with gifts and their love. Lucille worked at Macy's and Rose was a seamstress in the garment industry. They pooled some of their minimal earnings to buy us many of the more expensive toys we had as children. They gave me my first real two-wheeler, a blue and silver balloon-tired Rollfast bicycle, complete with light, reflectors, a speedometer and a horn. They also gave me my first serious baseball glove, a Spalding first baseman's mitt. I used to oil that glove with special oil to soften it. They also took us to places in New York City, sometimes when they were on dates with the men who seemed to be around rather frequently, especially in Aunt Rose's case. I vividly recall a time when Aunt Lucille took me to visit a friend whose brother Dominick had Down's syndrome (we called it something else then). He was probably 30 or 40 years of age, but he played with me, and then we ate blueberry pie together. When he ate the pie he brought his head close to the plate on the table and quickly scooped it into his nearby mouth. I'd never seen this before.

At some point after many years with us, now that it was more acceptable, our aunts got their own apartment together. This was a new liberation. It wasn't far from where we lived, so they continued seeing my parents and regularly sitting for us. Eventually, Lucille married Andrew Dewarde, a wonderful and interesting person. Much later on, after Rose had dated Jim Christian and Mayo Armani and others, she married Peter Naccarato, a volatile and unpredictable man. He was a garment presser in the clothing industry. Peter seemed to have opinions about everything, even things he knew little about. He'd raise his voice as if to superimpose his opinions. I'd often visit Aunt Lucille in Flatbush when Uncle Andrew, Uncle Strike and Joe Ellis (cousin Marie's husband) were in Trinidad building airplane runways during World War II. We'd go to the movies and have Chinese food on Saturday and attend church on Sunday morning. Since she was living alone and didn't have children, she seemed to enjoy my visits. So did I.

My mother was closest to her sister Rose; they stayed close right up until my mother died. There was a youthful innocence, beauty, and unpretentiousness about Rose. Many men were attracted to her, including construction workers who'd whistle at her as she ran to the Seabeach subway station, usually late for her work. She was always extremely helpful to my mother as a sister and companion. To this day, at 97, Rose can still be naive and unpretentious, almost as if she doesn't get what's going on about her, though it's more likely this is because of her serious health problems as she ages.

When Rose and Peter and their two daughters lived on 42nd Street in Sunnyside, their apartment was one floor above. Some of my early teenage friends were quite taken with her good looks and her spirit. She always seemed to be rushing somewhere and always had a smile on her face. She was lithe and athletic and had long, slender legs. Later on in life, several of my closer buddies revealed that they sometimes used to masturbate thinking about her. So had I, even though the Catholic Church told us that masturbation was an "impure" act towards one's self, a mortal sin that we had to confess to the priest. After a while, I stopped confessing what didn't seem like such a mortal sin to me. Of course, even if Rose had been aware of any pubescent fantasies about her it was most unlikely she would have any interest in these innocent young boys.

Paradoxically, though Rose had such an effect on sexually aware boys, her husband Peter was apparently uninterested in her and was frequently on the prowl for other women, or at least that's what I gathered from overheard remarks between my parents. When my father learned of Peter's roaming, he took it upon himself to protect his wife's baby sister. First he'd say something to Peter, but that didn't do any good. Then he confronted these women in the neighborhood, trying to intimidate them and warning them to stay away from Peter. He may have discouraged one or two of them. But of course the women weren't the problem, Peter was. My father had absolutely no right to involve himself in matters between Rose and Peter, but that didn't stop him. He saw himself as Rose's surrogate father and protector. Eventually, after many domestic disputes and growing apart, Rose and Peter were divorced. They were both better off without each other and so were their two daughters, Francine (Serio, but remained Naccarato) and Joan (Anastasio).

My mother often told us about her difficult relationship with her own mother. Whenever she acted like a teenager, her mother applied Old World Italian standards and called her relatively out-of- control or non-traditional, frequently punishing her, including physical beatings. Apparently her mother never acted this way with my mother's three sisters, or at least Elizabeth, Lucille and Rose never mentioned it.

Maybe my mother was more rebellious and adventurous, and would not bow to the cane or her mother's will. Her sisters have hinted that my mother would do what she wanted, despite warnings and prior punishments. Apparently her sisters were more compliant. Elizabeth left home early to get married, and Lucille and Rose were much younger, and this may have magnified Phyllis's behavior in her mother's mind.

One example of her early rebelliousness took place at a picnic she went on with a young man named Frank Muzio, and couple of close, unmarried friends, Anna and Tom (his surname was Balbo, I do not know hers), who later became my godparents when I was baptized in June 1932. I always called them Aunt Anna and Uncle Tom.

This infamous picnic took place one spring day on Staten Island. Billie, Frank, Anna and Tom had taken the ferry from Manhattan to this countrified remote hamlet, the least populated fifth borough, then and now. While the four of them were having a wonderful picnic, Anna noticed an older woman dressed completely in black and carrying a long stick, walking in their direction. She asked my mother if that wasn't her mother, and my mother remarked it couldn't be. How would her mother know where they were and how would she have gotten there? After all, the picnic was a closely guarded secret.

As the woman got closer, it turned out that it was her mother. My mother couldn't believe this elderly immigrant woman had found her way to Staten Island. Saying little, her mother grabbed her and used the wooden stick to smack her, humiliating her in front of her recent beau and her friends. She then dragged my mother by the arm back to the ferry, leaving the others. She never explained or apologized. It took a while for my mother to get over this.

This happened at least eight or 10 years before my parents were married in 1928, and my mother was quite young, 12 years younger than my father. Clearly her mother did not approve of my mother going somewhere with others, especially an older man, without her mother's permission and without some sort of chaperone. And, he was divorced. My mother told my sister and me about this incident several times and my father also remembered it.

But, that's not the end of the story, only the first part. In 1944 or 1945, when my sister was about 14 or 15 she hung out with what my mother believed was a rough, cigarette-smoking, probably French-kissing group of adolescents. Perhaps my sister did more than this, but we'll never know. Maria and her buddies used to stand on Queens Boulevard, not far from the local funeral home and a Chinese restaurant. One evening my sister was up there without my mother's knowledge or permission. When my mother didn't know where Maria was, she marched up to that corner where she thought Maria would be, on that warm, summer evening, grabbed her only daughter and smacked her across the face with the back of her left hand, which had her large diamond engagement ring on the third finger. That ring hit my sister squarely on her nose, sending blood gushing. At that time, shortly before Maria had plastic surgery to make it more pert, more American, this was a classic attractive Roman nose, similar to my mother's. When my mother and sister came back to the apartment, only a couple of blocks from the corner, my sister's nose was still bleeding and her blouse was covered in blood. It took a while for her nose to stop bleeding. No one ever questioned my mother's judgment or her right to do this, and we rarely discussed it again. But Maria never forgot this incident—how could she?—and probably has told the story to her own children, David Owen and Barbara Jane.

The third part of this mother/daughter punitive trilogy occurred many years later, when Maria was living in Larchmont, New York, an upper middle class community with high standards and pretenses, and where the children attended Mamaroneck High School in the adjacent town. Like her mother before her, Maria was concerned that Barbara Jane was hanging out with the wrong crowd, which Maria called "the greasers." This was the code word for the predominantly Italian-American boys who seemed to be going nowhere, at least according to my sister, despite the fine academic opportunities they had. Ironically, this group was probably quite similar to the one Maria had hung around with on Queens Boulevard those many years before. My sister kept a careful eye on Barbara Jane and once found her sitting on the schoolyard wall with a group of greasers. Maria went over to Barbara Jane, pulled her off the low wall and smacked Barbara Jane, right in front of her friends.

Apparently certain patterns repeat themselves and it doesn't take a psychologist or a sociologist to see a correlation among these three acts of public humiliation. My mother had a volatile relationship with her mother, and she had a similar relationship with her own daughter. Maria's relationship with her daughter also was occasionally volatile, but it was much more nurturing and loving.

If my sister Maria were somehow magically here right now, I'm confident her views of our mother would sharply contrast with mine. Although she had strongly negative feelings about our mother, she was far more tolerant of our father's behavior. Long after our mother was dead, Maria could still easily spew out her litany of complaints and harsh remarks about her and their tumultuous relationship. Maria had an uneven relationship with her creative son David but had far less controversy with her lovely and unpretentious daughter Barbara Jane.

Although my sister gave the distinct impression that she disliked our mother intensely, the word "angry" is probably more accurate. During Maria's teenage years and beyond they had ongoing clashes about even trivial issues. There was no doubt our mother was harsher with Maria than she was with me, finding it difficult to understand Maria's transgressions or her efforts to break out independently. Though my mother's words to Maria were too sharp, I am not sure she meant them. When anyone asked her about this, she would play innocent, saying that Maria had misunderstood.

My mother treated Maria forever as a child, never accepting her as a full-fledged adult, and criticizing almost everything Maria did. Our mother could never relinquish control and help Maria become independent. Therefore, strong-willed Maria constantly battled with her, never resolving the issues or finding harmony and understanding. This became a lifetime battle, with neither one yielding any ground. I never understood this ongoing war because our mother seemed so capable of getting along with her sisters and others who were certainly no more perfect or compliant than Maria.

Maria complained I was treated much better than she was because I was a son, the only one. She was right. Mother did treat me more kindly and gently than Maria and I did benefit from this discrimination. My mother's attitude reflected her deep Italian beliefs that male members of the family should be respected, obeyed and given primary attention. I had so much more freedom than Maria. I was allowed to stay out later at night without being asked where I would be going or when I would return. When I came home late as a teenager, there were no follow-up questions. When we were young, Maria would sometimes call me a "goody two shoes" because I always did the right thing and never got in trouble. This wasn't true at all. I just got away with a lot more than she did. Our mother was far more lenient with me when things did go awry. Maria was under much closer surveillance, and she was in the spotlight far more than I was, but she also found highly imaginative ways of getting out of the spotlight and doing what she wanted.

Because my mother could take shorthand and type extremely well, she was always able to find a job in some white-collar organization. These were not high-ranking or high-paying positions, but they were jobs and she did them well. Perhaps this is why it was important for her to teach me to touch-type. She purchased a Royal portable manual typewriter (that's all there was in those days) during the early years of World War II. We kept it in a sturdy leather carrying case. I remember spending many nights when she explained the importance of proper finger placement on the keys. She had a lesson book that she used to instruct me. There were all sorts of drills and repetitive combinations of the various letters. The theme was finger placement, memorization of the keys and practice, practice, practice. Then, we eventually moved on to actual English words, phrases and sentences. I kept that typewriter well into the mid 1950s, still using it through the summer of 1955 when I worked as a busboy with Jerry Pagano, Frank Grant (no relation to Lois) and Morty Greenberg at the Forest House in Lake Mahopac, New York. It was during that time I began to recognize my love for writing and spent time putting together short tales, descriptions of events occurring at the Forest House and long letters to dear friends.

With my mother's help and lots of practice, I got my first full time job as a typist for the Babee Tenda Corporation on Queens Boulevard in Elmhurst, Queens. After graduating from Long Island City High School, I worked there from January through August 1950, earning $35 a week (and took home $31.07) for 40 hours of work. One of the first things I did with an early paycheck was to go into Manhattan and buy a pair of thick-soled heavy cordovan shoes from Flag Brothers Shoe store, I felt so grown up. While typing in the Babee Tenda glass-front building, I often heard my friend Larry Sullivan and his buddy Mickey Quinn screaming out my name as they rode by on the bus to Rockaway Beach, everybody in the office heard them. No matter how many times I asked them not to do this, they wouldn't stop, taunting me for being at work while they went to the beach and to be with our friends.

My typing skills were extremely helpful when I had to write term papers at college, reports in the military, graduate school assignments and eventually scholarly papers as a college professor. All of this came pouring out of that Royal portable typewriter, along with letters to friends, newspapers or politicians, and the typing I did for others. Today, I'm still able to type accurately and fast, except now I do it on a computer, which speeds up the process considerably.

When my mother was still teaching me, she gave me quotations from famous people and had me type them for practice. This also must have been my mother's way to expose me to the words and thoughts of writers she respected, including Aldous Huxley, Robert Louis Stevenson, Albert Einstein, Shakespeare, John Stuart Mill and Michel de

Montaigne. Surprisingly, I still have some of those typed quotations on worn 3 by 5 cards in my desk.

One of these cards contains the words an English professor wrote on a paper I had submitted, which I later typed on a card when I was a freshman at Columbia in the fall of 1950. I was 18, uncertain and nervous about being at Columbia, not sure I deserved to be there. At the beginning of the fall semester, this professor asked the class to write about what they had done over the summer. He obviously wanted to determine whether we could write at college level, or the areas we might need improvements.

Along with the other 12-15 freshmen, I wrote for almost the entire hour, explaining how, after being too shy for more than two years I'd finally asked Jeanette Dunphy, a classmate from Long Island City High School for a date. When I did call her and asked if she'd go to Jones Beach next Sunday, she remarked, "I never thought you'd call." We had a wonderful summer dating, regularly going to Jones Beach, the movies and church in her parish. At the end of the writing exercise focusing on the past summer, I apologetically wrote on my paper, "I do not think that this is the best I can do." I was defending myself and apologizing even before there was any reason to do it. Several days later when the professor returned my paper to the class, he'd made grammatical corrections, and gave me an A-minus. Most important to me, he wrote the words I later typed on to the card, saved, and still have:

"At the last Judgment we are all going to make the same remark. But some of us are going to the mansions prepared for us from the beginning; the rest will go to Hell, and there will be no appeal. However, I think this paper is satisfactory and in places very good. Besides, this isn't the last judgment, is it?"

A long time ago, Henry Adams said: "A teacher touches eternity; he can never tell where his influence stops." It's now 57 years since I wrote that paper and I will never know how many ways, that young English professor L.D. Maher, affected my life. His thoughtful, provocative words gave me much needed support for the rest of my freshman year and beyond. Why else would I have kept them all these years?

In the middle of my junior year at Columbia, I transferred to Queens College. My father had started to show some early signs of illness, and I was worried about the rising tuition costs at Columbia. I thought $16 dollars per course credit was excessive and worried where I would find the money if my father became seriously ill. So I decided to transfer to a public college that had free tuition for qualified New York City residents. I never consulted my parents on this; I just did it. Queens College turned out to be a fine institution, with many outstanding professors, an excellent balanced curriculum, solid courses and extremely high academic standards.

Bob Wilson and I were classmates at Queens, although I'd known him for several years. One day he told us his mother was in the hospital for an emergency appendectomy. We already know that my mother worried about people getting enough food and loved to feed them. Although she did not know Mrs. Wilson, my mother suggested that I bring Bob home with me for supper. Bob waited for me to finish up in one of the late afternoon Bio labs. Then we hitchhiked the two miles from Queens College to our house a few miles further out in Flushing.

On these journeys, we talked incessantly about every conceivable topic, most frequently about sports and young girls at the college, and books. We double-dated a lot, going to the Central Plaza for jazz concerts in lower Manhattan, and played on the varsity baseball team together along with another dear friend, George Rooney. Sports were important competitive activities, and I was fortunate to have played football at Columbia and track, baseball and some soccer at Queens. Somehow, I strived to be a better athlete through intense physical efforts and a sheer desire to win, especially in the track meets.

I guess Bob liked my mother's cooking. For the next six weeks, he continued coming home with me for dinner every weekday evening and sometimes on weekends. Bob was slender and solidly built, he could eat endlessly while remaining slender, and that's exactly what he did for those six weeks. Even my mother said he sure could eat a lot. By about the fifth week, my mother asked me how much longer Bob's mother would be in the hospital. The next day he told me she'd been home for several weeks, and had stayed there only a week or so after her emergency appendectomy operation. When I asked him why he hadn't said anything sooner, he said that my mother was so much better cook than his, and the meals were more hearty and satisfying, he figured he would just keep coming over for dinner for as long as he could.

This happened right after a meal when Bob and I had consumed the better part of a 4-½ pound roast beef. After that, my mother told me to tell Bob it was time for him to return to his apartment in Woodside for whatever meals his own mother was cooking. Bob smiled and accepted his fate without complaint. It wasn't the last meal Bob had at our house, though somehow he still managed to come over after classes once in a while. I recently reminded Bob of his dinner adventures. He said he remembered it quite well, although he denies that it lasted so many weeks. I trust my mother on this number, but she might have exaggerated a bit.

I graduated from Queens College in February 1955 and stayed on at the college working as an apprentice to George Riddock, the school's carpenter, while applying to various medical schools. I learned a great deal about carpentry along with George's views on just about everything else in life. George was originally from Aberdeen Scotland, and once you got past his pronounced Scottish accent, you realized what a profound, astute thinker he was. There wasn't any subject he didn't have views about. He was also well informed about our country and offered reasonable criticisms of politics. I worked with George for a while before deciding to fulfill my military service obligation instead of going to medical school.

The military draft was still in effect and my 2-S student deferment was now over. If I didn't choose to enlist, I would have been drafted into the Army. I definitely did not want that. Although my close childhood friend Larry Sullivan was going into the Air Force to become a pilot, he urged me to apply for the officer candidate program in the United States Marine Corps. Larry explained to me the various advantages of the Marine Corps, including the esprit de corps, and where the various Marine bases are located. I formally enlisted in the United States Marine Corps in the winter of 1956. In preparation for this experience, I'd religiously worked out doing all kinds of strenuous exercises and running miles each day to be in outstanding shape before reporting for duty.

A month or so before leaving for the Marine Corps, I took a car trip to Florida with another dear friend, Ed Greeley. While driving through Georgia, we saw a totally black prison chain gang, guarded by a heavy-set man on horseback holding a rifle. The prisoners looked at us as we slowly drove by them. Neither of us had ever seen a chain gang, we thought they didn't exist anymore. Then, we stopped down the road and we took out the 22-caliber rifle Ed had brought with us and fired a bunch of rounds into the woods. We were both quiet for a while. What firing that rifle meant is still unclear. When we were starting out this trip, and when my father kissed me goodbye, he noticed the rifle in Ed's car and was upset with this. Ed thought we needed some sort of protection on our voyage.

On our way home, one of our goals was to visit Asheville, North Carolina, which had been the home of author Thomas Wolfe (not Tom Wolfe, another author who's still alive). Ed and I were great devotees of Wolfe's writing. In Asheville we met Wolfe's sister Mabel and visited Wolfe's home where his mother had run a boarding house. While there at night I would hear the lonely wailing of the railroad trains in the surrounding mountains, and I thought of Wolfe's detailed descriptions of these sounds. Parts of Asheville appeared to be just as Wolfe had described it in his novels.

This was a pilgrimage for us and we talked about Wolfe a lot on the way to and from Florida. Even as the years went by, neither of us could understand why Wolfe never seemed to get the adoration and scholarly attention of other contemporary American authors such as Hemingway, Fitzgerald or Steinbeck. Perhaps it was because he died so young, he had tuberculosis of the brain, just before his 38th birthday, and had published only two major novels. Since Wolfe left large crates of his longhand writing, his editors were able to publish several of his books posthumously. Perhaps some day a larger audience will appreciate his place in American literature. Over the years I have become a Thomas Wolfe expert. I've read just about everything he wrote, his letters, plays and those posthumously published works, along with many criticisms of his writings. His extended descriptions of just about anything and the development of his fictional characters have always interested me. A major criticism of Wolfe's writing has been he is too wordy, and I have been told the same thing. Ed Greeley also died relatively young from cancer on April 15, 1997. Each spring when income taxes are due, I especially think of Ed and what a fine person he was. Both before and after that date, my parents and sister also died in the spring, but I will deal with these later on.

In March 1956, there was a major blizzard in New York, just as my mother and I took the subway from Flushing to the train station for my longer journey to Marine Corps training in Quantico, Virginia. We didn't say much to one another on the ride from Flushing. At Penn Station, we kissed and hugged and quietly parted after she reminded me to be careful and take care of myself. I had already hugged and kissed my father at home, and he had also told me to be safe and don't volunteer for anything. In my suitcase I had several books I planned to read while in the officer training program. Little did I realize then there would be absolutely no time to read or do anything but to focus on becoming a Marine.

Because of blizzard, which affected the whole East Coast, I arrived late at Quantico, Virginia. This was a major, inexcusable, outright mistake and I should have left much earlier. It was the beginning of my some initial difficulties.

When I arrived at the station along with other late arrivals, we were met by a sharp looking, perfectly sculptured Marine with brown Smokey Bear cap bearing the Marine Corps symbol. He stood there by the tracks in an immaculately pressed uniform and spit-shined cordovan shoes with a clipboard in his hands. In accented English I couldn't identify, he yelled at us, demanded to know where we'd been. He hollered at us to board a waiting truck after we threw our baggage up in it. When some stragglers were slow responding to this order, this taut and screaming person threw some bags on his own. When we arrived at camp, I was taken into an office and told to stand "nose and toes" to the wall. I'd never heard this term, but quickly learned that it meant standing with your nose directly against the wall and your feet touching the baseboard. We stood there for what seemed to be hours (Lois, the woman I would marry a year and a half later doubted it was this long). There I was, completely unaware of what would happen, whether I would live or possibly die. Nobody cared if my bladder was full, or that I was sweating in that hot office wearing the wool sweater my mother had given me. It was if I wasn't even there for hours.

Nobody had ever treated me this way, no parent or nun, no coach, no supervisor, no friend or foe, nobody. At one point I was sure I would reflexively urinate and probably receive some other severe punishment, but somehow didn't. Eventually someone came over to me, asked my name and hollered directly in my ear to get out of his sight and report to a nearby building. I had learned the unwritten Marine rule: "When you're on time, you're late." Ever since then I always strive to be on time and often think of that initial experience.

Soon my fellow Officer Candidate Program members and I were regularly subjected to almost the same rigorous training as enlisted recruits at Parris Island or San Diego. I think they modified some of the training just a bit to ensure that potential officers didn't wash out in large numbers, but even so, some of the men (only Caucasian males and a handful of male candidates from South Korea were in the program then) did not succeed, some couldn't meet the rigorous physical standards, some broke down mentally and physically, and disappeared. I still remember some of their faces and names.

Our platoon learned from – and survived the sadistic behavior of—Drill Sergeant Wolfgang Klaus Rother, a former member of the German army, the same man who had met we stragglers at the train station. With his typical crisp Aryan features, Rother looked like a chiseled German soldier, maybe even an SS member, though now he wore a Marine uniform. Despite the scrutiny of any officers, he found cunning ways to do strange and harassing things to us when they were out of sight. Some of us thought he was out of his mind but barely dared to say so, at least never above a whisper to each other. Sgt. Rother's sole pleasure and purpose in life was to harass our platoon members constantly and unexpectedly, day and night. He was responsible for a half-dozen college graduate candidates flunking out, and he did it with glee. Once he found a weak spot or fear, he became a raging predatory animal who would go after you until he brought you down. He wanted us to think he was doing a great service for both the Marine Corps and the weak candidate, but he clearly cared only for the Marine Corps. In his mixed English-German accent he would incessantly remind us of looking "goddamn sharp." Sometimes my buddy Jim Reno and I would privately imitate his unique accent and burst out laughing. One of my major goals was to stay out of Sgt. Rother's mind and sight, and I became a successful, and in some respects, an outstanding candidate.

Completing the Officer Candidate Program was the finest training experience I ever had. Besides learning a great deal about becoming a Marine, I learned much about myself, my capacity to endure hardship, to work cooperatively with others, and to be a team player. I became more complete, independent and self-confident. I had survived some of the most harassing and physically grueling physical activities I ever had experienced. Even though I had played various sports in school and in the neighborhood and vigorously trained for all of them, they were relatively mild by comparison. You were pushed to unknown limits, far beyond any pre-conceived notions you had about yourself.

Overcoming adversity, suffering the pain of the field exercises and long hikes and running, being exhausted yet continuing beyond my imagined limits made me a better person. You learned to support your Marine buddies, and they did the same for you. I developed leadership skills and was seen as a sound leader. I love the Marine Corps, and I came to know and love my Marine buddies, even those I was not always fond. The Marine Corps motto, Semper Fidelis, always faithful, has always appealed to me. I still subscribe to the Marine Corps traditions, the concept of "no excuse," the commitment to duty, mission, excellence and service. To this day, I consider any Marine, enlisted or officer, a member of my "band of brothers." There is no finer organization in the world. The expression "once a Marine, always a Marine" is real. In recent years, the Marine Corps slogan has been, "The Change is Forever," and that's true for me. Succeeding in the Marine Corps was my Mount Everest. Even up to today the Marine Corps has been a profound influence on my life and behavior.

I still stay in touch with my buddy Jim Reno, a Notre Dame graduate from Michigan. As officer candidates we used to talk endlessly while sitting on our locker boxes, spit-shining our boots and shoes. (According to Jim, though, he only listened endlessly.) Jim and his wife Patricia live in Lake Arrowhead, where Lois and I have visited with them. Since several 3-56 Basic School reunions, we've met other buddies we'd not seen or spoken to in almost 50 years. Sometimes a group of us titled the Eastern Strategists meet in Princeton for lunch, or dinner with our wives. We discuss each other's lives, politics, the world, anything we want to in an open and unpretentious way. Civility, humor and clarity prevail. Junction Alexander, Tony Dunleavy, Tom Regan, Tom Agnew and recently Frank Gargano along with me form this bonding group. Each year we have a dinner with our wives to celebrate the United States Marine Corps' birthday and we sing the Marine Corps Hymn.

It was pouring rain on graduation day at Quantico in June 1956 when we were to be commissioned as Second Lieutenants, and they kept our class waiting in the rain for a long time outside the main base auditorium. We were wearing our perfectly fitting new green winter officers' uniforms covered by Marine green, full-length, water-repellent raincoats and covers on our caps. It was as if we had to endure one final degrading and inconvenient experience just before we had our gold, Second Lieutenant bars fixed to our dress jackets and shirts and sworn in as officers.

While we were waiting in the rain, some of us noticed a lone civilian woman about 150 yards away walking towards us under an umbrella. As she got closer, her gait, size and style told me it was my mother, Phyllis, Billie Muzio. I ran up to her and we hugged. She had never told me she was coming. After she had received a formal invitation from the base commander to attend the graduation ceremony, as did other parents and spouses she decided to go. So she traveled from Northport, Long Island to Penn Station, taking a train to Washington, D.C. followed by another train to Quantico, Virginia. In the town of Quantico, she showed a cab driver the invitation and he drove her to where he thought it was being held. He was wrong, and left her about a half mile from the auditorium. So she inquired and then dauntlessly walked the rest of the way in the rain with her trusty umbrella.

I was overwhelmed. But that was my mother, always the Rock. She told me my father couldn't be there because he had become increasingly ill from the disease that eventually led to his death; its name was never mentioned. It was an honor for me that she was there to see me become a Marine officer. After all, I thought she was so old, all of 53 years of age although in excellent health and spirits. But to me at 24, she seemed terribly old then. After the ceremonies and a brief reception, she and I drove back to New York in my trusty, cramped Volkswagen Beetle, full of all my military gear and a footlocker. Back home I visited my ailing father who still was unaware of the dimensions of his changing health. He only knew he wasn't feeling well, what he called "peculiar" and somewhat weak.

After a week or so of leave I returned to Quantico for another eight months of advanced officer training, which I completed in the winter of 1957. There were 557 men (no women) in my basic class, 3-56 BC, divided into three companies, Echo, Foxtrot and Golf. For the rest of the program I lived in a Quonset hut with 43 other officers from all over the country and with remarkably different personalities and interests. Some of them went home at night, they were married and a few had children, and were referred to as "brown baggers." One of our classmates and a friend, Jack Ruppert, recently wrote a fine analytical book about our basic class and those since then, called *One of Us, Officers of Marines, Their Training, Traditions, and Values.*

Because I did well in Basic School, the Marines granted my request for duty to be stationed at Camp Pendleton California, where I served as a Platoon Infantry Officer. After some time in Queens, I made the cross-country trip in my trusty Volkswagen Beetle from New York to Southern California by way of Asheville, North Carolina, where I picked up my traveling companion, Hugh Stephens, a fellow Marine. I was back in Thomas Wolfe's hometown. We took the southern route, assisted by a series of maps from Texaco in a spiral binder, which another Marine, Jack McGivney, had helped us acquire. We completed the trip in six or seven days, driving about 400-500 miles a day, chatting about our lives.

Though we traveled on smoothly paved highways and clearly marked roads, I saw myself as some sort of modern day adventurer. Whenever we stopped for gas or food, or had to use the toilet, people were amazed to see my beetle-shaped German car. Even though some Volkswagens had started showing up in the late 1940s and early 1950s, they were still relatively rare outside big cities, and many people had never seen anything like them. They asked all sorts of questions about this strange vehicle. What about gas mileage? Did it ever break down? (No.) How fast could I go? (65 miles per hour, maybe more, depending on the road). They were amazed when they discovered that the 36-horsepower, air-cooled engine was in the back of the car instead of the front where all other auto engines were; and that the gas tank was under the hood in the front.

Hugh was unhappy during our cross-country journey. He'd been married after we finished Basic School at Quantico, and it seemed unfair to him that he was shipping out to Okinawa, while I was a bachelor going to lovely southern California. He probably was right, but that was the USMC's way of doing things and there was no way to question the decision. When we arrived in California, I dropped Hugh off at the Los Angeles train station, shook hands and hugged him, then headed to Pendleton, south of Los Angeles. Pendleton is a massive, 125,000-acre base with lots of Pacific Ocean waterfront and endless rolling hills, between San Diego and many attractive beach towns, including San Clemente and Laguna Beach. I remember seeing palm trees, and the smell of oranges in the air, along with a breeze carrying the salt air from the nearby Pacific Ocean.

In the early 2000s, I saw Hugh Stephens at a 3-56 Marine Corps reunion. Hugh had become a dean at a leading university. When I mentioned our cross-country trip to him, he said he didn't remember complaining about being sent to Okinawa instead of Pendleton. But this was almost 50 years later. The years do change our thinking and memory.

Later on at Pendleton, I was a "gung ho" platoon commander L. Company, 3rd Battalion, 5th Marine Regiment in charge of 44 young enlisted Marines from all over the country, including eight or nine full-blooded American Indians. I placed the following quotation above the barracks entrance:

"I have just returned from the front and seen the finest fighting organization the world has ever known, the United States Marine Corps."

General of the Army, Douglas MacArthur

In September of 1957 I returned to the East Coast from Camp Pendleton to marry Lois Ann Grant. We were married on September 21, 1957 at the Hollis Congregational Church in Queens Village Queens. Later that month I reported to the Naval Ordnance Base in Indianhead, Maryland to train as an Explosives Ordnance Disposal Officer. Apparently, someone had determined I was psychologically fit for this hazardous work, learning to disarm bombs, artillery shells, mines and other armament. But, I did volunteer for it and have nobody but myself to blame. Volkswagen Beetles were hot sales items on the West Coast, so I could have sold it, and have some extra money after paying $150 to fly home. Instead, I loaded my car with Marine Corps food rations and much of my property and drove solo back across America. I made the trip in just under 4 ½ days, driving 18 or 19 hours a day, stopping only for the toilet and gasoline. It was a long, lonely and exhausting trip, one I should have avoided if my decision had been a sounder one.

I could say a lot more about the 3-1/2 years I spent in the Marine Corps, but I'll save that for another time. I want this memoir to concentrate mostly on my parents and my family.

Shortly after getting to Queens I had a major auto accident a few blocks from Lois's house after we were returning from purchasing our wedding rings at the jewelry exchange in Manhattan. It was totally my fault. Because of my inattention and exhaustion from my alone cross-country trip, Lois ended up with a broken wrist. My face was marred by cuts from the broken windshield. The windshield in a Volkswagen Beetle was extremely close to the driver and front passenger. The accident threw Lois against the dashboard. She had been carrying two one-quart cardboard milk containers on her lap, maybe by cushioning her they acted like our more modern air bag. Even so, I thought for an instant I maimed her for life, or worse. When my mother saw us shortly after the accident, she abruptly queried, "How could you do this to me?" just as she had done so many years earlier when I had the ice skating accident as a youngster in Brooklyn. Once again it was if it was some intentional incident seemingly to her detriment.

Both of us looked like damaged goods at our wedding and Lois had to leave some of the buttons on the sleeve of her wedding dress open for her injured wrist. Our wedding pictures, taken a few days after the accident, required extensive touching up to mask the damage. Our faithful Volkswagen was now undrivable and we borrowed another one from my best man Larry Sullivan and his wife Maureen for our journey to Washington, D.C. Once there, we quickly found a furnished apartment at 620 Alabama Avenue, S.E. It was our first apartment and it was lovely. It also a block or so from St. Elizabeth's Hospital, a federal mental institution where Lois went to work the next week as a nurse, she'd recently graduated from the Roosevelt Hospital School of Nursing in Manhattan and would be working full time while I was attending Explosives Ordnance Disposal School.

Grandma Muzio & son Joseph

Frank Muzio as a
very young man

Frank Muzio as a
young man

Frank Muzio (on right) with army buddies in France,
World War I

Phyllis Brancata Muzio on her wedding day

Frank and Phyllis Muzio
at Racetrack

Frank and Phyllis Muzio
in Florida

Frank and Phyllis with children Joseph and Maria

Frank and Phyllis dancing later in life

CHAPTER IV

FRANK'S JOURNEY

My father, Frank Muzio, was born February 28, 1891, he died April 27, 1958. I have not found any immigration or naturalization documents regarding his birth location.

My father's complete origins and most of his earlier life is a mystery. Compared to my mother's life, we know almost nothing about my father's early years, barely bits and pieces. For example, until this time, I had not known completely if my father was born in Italy or in the United States. My editor did uncover a ship manifest indicating his name and birthdate, and his coming to America on a ship Citta di Napoli. His birth location on the manifest is listed as Potenza. Some relatives have told me they thought my father was born in Manhattan, but others were uncertain. His father, Nicholas (Nicolas) was a rag picker in Italy though we don't know how he could earn a living from this trade. Nicholas died at age 42 and we know little more about him. Since there were no discussions of him when we were growing up, I've wondered whether he lived with the rest of the family. The Muzio family definitely came from a poor town in southern Italy, Craco, in the province of Basilicata, north of the Bay of Taranto, the arch of the Italy's geographic boot.

When Lois and I were in Italy in the spring 2007 I'd planned to seek more info on his birthplace and my mother's, but I gave up on this idea. I decided it didn't matter at this point and it would have little bearing on the thrust of this memoir.

My father was the third of four, possibly five children; his sister Theresa was older, Carmela was younger, and his brother, Joseph, who was older, died at 34, as I describe below. Aunt Theresa or Tessie married a man named Marrona and they had at least four children. Aunt Carmela's married name was Mormando, and she had nine sons and one daughter (that's right), she was called "Babe." My father once told me his sister Carmela used to buy rubber hose by the foot length because she used it to sometimes smack her supposedly out of control nine sons, usually after she chased them down. In preparatory protection, they would hide the hose to prevent this, but she'd buy another length to carry out her concept of effective child rearing. Except for cousin Rocco who was my age, they were all older, and as a child I thought they were loud and fun loving. Some of them had occasional confrontations with the local police. As a little boy, I remember visiting my father's mother, Caterina Santa Lucia Muzio, at her home in Brooklyn. Aunt Tessie and Aunt Camela also lived in Brooklyn, but I believe towards the end portion of her life, my grandmother lived in Aunt Tessie's house.

Earlier, I briefly described my father's appearance. My father's face was broad, with a most distinct jaw line and broad nose, along with the clearest, most beautiful hazel eyes I had ever seen. Sometimes they seemed to be clear green, other times gray, occasionally almost smoky. When he smiled, his face had an open, inviting look; and when he was serious or angry, it took on a tense, penetrating stare that made you wonder what was he thinking, or what was he going to do. Both my mother and father had distinct ways of looking at you, directly, deeply and warmly, holding you focused on their expressive, clear eyes. You were drawn to their faces, at least I was.

My father was short but had an athletic, lean appearance, and was mostly bald except for a rim of hair that turned from brown to gray as he aged. He had probably been bald from his late twenties, certainly by the time he returned from France after serving in the U.S. Army in the First World War. I don't think his weight ever varied more than a couple of pounds, except late in his life when he was gravely ill and dying. His shoulders were broad, and his arms were more fully developed than one would expect for a man of his size and weight. As a child I remember staring at his powerful arms and his large hands when I was sitting next to him and he was driving us somewhere. I'm sure that his early life as an apprentice to a blacksmith and his similar military assignment in World War I were the sources of these powerful upper body, shoulders and arms.

Throughout his life my father was an excellent physical specimen. He always kept himself meticulously clean and wore French shaving lotions. He cared about his appearance, dressing in clothes that emphasized his athletic, trim body (including what were known as French-cut boxer shorts). In his earlier years he had his nails manicured on a regular basis, another example of special attention he gave himself. He knew he was attractive and jokingly reminded us how "handsome" he was. He claimed that women would bite the insides of their lips when they saw him, but of course we thought he was making some sort of joke. Or was it?

For a man his size, he was incredibly strong. When he was younger he worked out on the gymnastic apparatus of parallel bars, the horse and the swinging rings. For a while he was an amateur prizefighter. All this intense athletic activity helped him maintain a taut physical perfection, broad-shouldered and thin waisted

It was always easy for us to recognize my father's unique gait. He walked with a hurried prance, alert, always moving quickly, but gracefully, his body erect and shoulders back, as if he were on some important mission. He almost seemed to be in a military parade.

Most of what I know about my father comes from photographs, a few other documents, my remembrances of events and conversations, and from talking with my remaining, older relatives, including my mother's youngest sister, 97-year-old Aunt Rose and particularly my cousin Henry Buono Jr. now 87. Henry, who became a decorated pilot in World War II, knew my father even before he was married to my mother, and long before my sister and I were born. In fact, he knew my father when he was married to his first wife, not my mother, the one I never heard about until much later in my life. From his stories, it's clear that Henry idolized my father, and in turn my father served as a mentor to him. Neither Rose nor Henry could tell me much about my paternal grandfather, but maybe they just don't remember. Still, it seems strange that we know so little about him.

When my father was young, his older brother Joseph had a failing kidney, or some related illness. Each morning before school my father had to take a trolley to some other part of the city to get a pail of goat's milk for his sick brother. No one seems to know the value of goat's milk for an ailing urinary system or who prescribed this questionable cure. Sometimes the round trip took longer than it should have, making my father late for school. Eventually and unfortunately, in the sixth grade he was thrown out of school for his continual lateness. Joseph eventually died in 1913 after being ill for many years. He was about 33 or 34.

Shortly after being thrown out of school, my father somehow got a job as an apprentice to a neighborhood blacksmith. Being on the streets of Manhattan as a youngster without parental control and little involvement decidedly shaped and also scarred his life, and the streets were his primary schoolroom. He became a street-savvy child and was always wary. It's difficult to know what a 12-year-old did in a blacksmith shop, but you did what you were told. Some things you were taught by the blacksmith, some you learned by trial and error experiences. There were no child labor laws, minimal wages or job benefits in the early 1900s. Other than his apprenticeship in blacksmithing and some adult education courses in public speaking that he took later in life, my father had little formal schooling. He was painfully aware of his educational inadequacies; as an adult he did the reading of self-improvement books to partially offset his recognized shortcomings.

Many years later, as each of our three sons finished the sixth grade and being 12, I couldn't help comparing their lives with my father's. Could Frank, Edward or Matthew survive on the streets with just a sixth-grade education? Could I have? Obviously the answer is consistently "No." But, sadly, stories like my father's were rather common at that time in this country.

When I asked my father about his apprenticeship with the blacksmith, he told me it was hard work, long hours, and poor wages, but he learned a lot about working with metal. The blacksmithing trade was more than shoeing horses and fixing wagon wheels and related equipment. My father also learned how to care for and understand the horses that came into the blacksmith shop. He told us that shoeing a horse was far more complicated and potentially dangerous than one might imagine. For example, he had to learn to stand calmly and quietly next to the horse and correctly lift a hoof off of the ground, thereby making it impossible for the horse to kick him or to buck on the three grounded legs. He told us that horses are difficult and unpredictable animals, each with its own personality. But he eventually learned to work successfully and devotedly with them, even how to break them to harness and saddle.

My father loved talking about horses, caring for them and admiring them. He must have transmitted his love of horses to me, because I too loved them. As a child in Sunnyside Queens I used to rush home for lunch and leave time to stop and pet the Sheffield Farm milk wagon horse I regularly saw on 43rd Avenue, sometimes giving it an apple or carrot or sugar lump before I returned to school. On my bedroom wall I had pasted the photographs of all the horses that had won the Kentucky Derby. I memorized all of their names, their jockeys and the year they won. When our parents took us to racetracks my sister and I would go in the paddock area to pet the race horses if the owners would let us.

My father later was drafted into the army in about 1916 or 1917, but had some initial problems at his induction physical, probably because of his personality, his cleanliness habits and his respect for his body. After waiting for what seemed like forever, it was his turn to stand almost naked in front of the physician, who tested his eyes, heart and teeth, then turned to other parts including his rectum. When the doctor told my father to drop his French silk underwear and bend over, my father objected and refused to do so. He'd already noticed the physician did not wash his hands after examining the rectums of the other inductees before examining my father. This was unacceptable to him.

When my father demanded that the doctor first wash his hands, the doctor and the other officers quickly conferred and told him he was disobeying a direct order and would be subject to a court martial and thrown in the stockade. My father reminded them that he wasn't in the army yet. The doctor reluctantly acquiesced. He did wash his hands. We'll never know if the doctor continued washing his hands between next examinations, but he did it for Frank Muzio, and that was my father's sole concern. Let the others speak for themselves.

In one of many of our conversations over the years Dad had told me while in the army, he had important, vital military assignments, and there weren't many others could do his job. Of course that wasn't so, there were probably many hundreds of thousands of horses used in World War I and thousands of soldiers assigned to care for them.

Once in the army he went to Camp Upton on Long Island, where he was classified a "Wagoner." Because he'd been a blacksmith, being given responsibility for the horses assigned to his unit was the perfect assignment. His duties included caring for the horses and tending to their stables and equipment. When he was shipped to France, he would take the horses the army had bought or confiscated, shoe them, and then break them for various needs, such as pulling artillery pieces and other heavy equipment and gear, or for the officers to ride. These horses were vital to the entire war campaign. But the way he told the tale, he was the best. When he was in France with the famous Lost Battalion, the 308th Regiment, 77th Division, he had to help slaughter some of their horses so they could eat when there were diminishing regular food supplies. Years later, during World War II, he would sometimes tell us these same stories as we ate the horsemeat he'd brought home for his family when there were the normal meat shortages. His white marble tombstone at the National Cemetery in Farmingdale, Long Island, bears only his name and a single word: "Wagoner."

We never knew what my father did after World War I ended on Armistice Day, November 11, 1918. Only recently my cousin Henry told me that my father stayed in France for almost a year after the war. Knowing he'd spent a year in France solves the mystery of why my father sometimes spoke brief coherent sentences in French. He tried to get my sister and me to say some of them. Why did he stay in France? Did he visit Paris? How did he earn a living there? No one seems to know these answers, another puzzle about my father.

My father did have visible souvenirs of his army duty in France, a large tattoo on each well-defined forearm, which had faded somewhat by the time I saw them as a young child. I remember that one of the tattoos was a large crucifix, with details of Christ in colors that emphasized the details, especially the crown of thorns on his head. I don't remember much about the other tattoo, but a second cousin has told me it also was a crucifix. I remember looking at the tattoos when my father held me in his arms, sometimes rubbing my hands over them and outlining the figures, wondering how they got there. When I asked him how they did tattooing my father went into great detail about the whole procedure, just as he did on the many other topics he knew about. Over the years, my father told us he was sorry he'd ever gotten tattooed, but at that time there was little he could do to remove them. He seldom wore short sleeve shirts because he didn't like showing the tattoos. He urged me never to get any. Following his advice, I never did.

The tattoos became even less distinct as my father's arms became thinner with aging and especially when he became ill with cancer. But I also remember looking at the long, branching blood vessels on his forearms that ran so clearly, just below the surface of his smooth, tight skin. It's as if they were some sorts of vital roadmap you could follow; and sometimes I did just that, gently running my small fingers along these bulges up and down his arms. Later, as he lay in the Veterans' Administration hospital shortly before he died, the staff still had no difficulty identifying a pronounced vessel for drawing blood or to insert an intravenous (IV) needle.

More surprising than the news about the year my father spent in France was Cousin Henry's telling me the details that he had been married to another woman, I think before and during the war, a woman named Lena Palughi who lived nearby in lower Manhattan. Henry told me my father had divorced her when he came back from the Army. In those days in New York State, adultery was the sole reason for divorce. So, apparently someone staged a situation to prove that his wife was sleeping with someone else. There's also the possibility she was doing this anyway. Once this was documented, the divorce was granted. No one in our family has ever seen such a document. If it ever existed, it's probably long lost. Besides cousin Henry's details, I had only found out about the divorce after my sister told me about it and long after my father died. I have no idea how she knew about it.

My father was always secretive; he told you only what he wanted you to know. Why didn't he tell us he'd been married before he left for the army in 1917, or that he'd divorced his first wife when he came back? Why didn't he ever tell us he'd stayed in France for a year after World War I and what did he do there? And why was there so much secrecy about his involvement in bookmaking and loan-sharking while he ran his various restaurants? Why did I find out these things only as a college student and much later on? He never gave answers to these questions and the implication of this is he must have kept other things from us.

My paternal grandmother Caterina Santa Lucia Muzio seemed tall and slender, probably because I was a child and everyone is taller to a child. But others in the family and some photographs show that she was taller than my father. I don't remember her speaking English, and she probably didn't, so she spoke only Italian with her children. We usually visited her Sunday afternoons after mass. We would always have a large, communal meal in the basement at a long, rectangular, marble table, sometimes covered with shiny oil cloth. I remember that every Sunday was the same with no variations: visit our grandmother and our nearby aunts, play with our cousins, then eat. Sometimes the men gambled in a garage, playing dice for money.

When I was about five and Maria was seven my father's mother became extremely ill. According to our family, grandma had cancer of the nose, and it was spreading to other parts of her face. When we visited her, she was always in bed. Someone would pick us up and have us kiss her when we arrived and when we left. We had no idea what was happening to her face, and our elders, with their lowered voices, seldom if ever used the word "cancer." Maybe they didn't know, or maybe they preferred to deny it. We were simply told she was sick. I still can recall the special medicinal odor of that dark upstairs bedroom.

In that room the heavy shades partly drawn, and there was a crucifix on the wall directly above her head. Our Sunday visits went on for what must have been months until grandma died. In those days, families waked their dead at home and I vaguely remember this happening with my grandmother, but it seems unlikely that children as young as we were went to the burial funeral.

My father was always in sound health and careful about his life, except for one glaring thing, the one that ultimately killed him: He smoked cigarettes. He spoke many times about quitting, but it never happened. He listened to my mother's nagging but heard nothing. When he had started smoking and thereafter, no one talked about addiction or habituation but he was a tobacco addict, smoking two packs a day. Nor did the government, the cigarette manufacturers, the advertisers, the medical professionals or anyone else ever mention any possible linkage between smoking, addiction, and a host of dangerous diseases, including lung and mouth cancer, bronchitis, upper respiratory infections, circulatory difficulties, and heart disease. Because he believed in the supposed pleasure and tension-relieving benefits of smoking, he preferred well-advertised, unfiltered, powerful Lucky Strike cigarettes.

Only years later did reports start coming out confirming a relationship between cigarette smoking and cancer. The initial reports were received with mixed beliefs and reactions, especially denials. Powerful cigarette companies and adroit advertising agencies effectively countered the initial reports on the deleterious effects of cigarettes. The correlation between cancer and smoking was to become a highly controversial scientific, health and legal issue. And there would be a major impact on the many businesses directly and indirectly related to the powerful tobacco industry in our country.

Only later, after more conclusive negative publicity and confirming data about cigarettes grew did my father switch to Parliaments with filters. Eventually he started using a cigarette holder that made use of disposable filter inserts. Once in a while providing us with instruction supporting cigarette damages, he would show us the darkened contaminated disposable filter before inserting a fresh one. Despite a long-term chronic hacking cough, and the need to frequently clear his throat, he still smoked and smoked, and yes, it killed him.

While he smoked for his entire adult life, my father urged his children never to smoke because it was a "dirty, nasty, habit." He never made a correlation between smoking and illness. Of course he had no idea his "habit" was a chemical addiction that could sicken or ultimately kill him. Sometimes when smoking, he would unfold a laundered handkerchief with his initials embroidered on it, draw deeply on the cigarette and, while holding the handkerchief to his lips, exhaled the hot smoke through it. The smoke left behind a brownish stain with tiny black specks in it. This was my father's lesson to us, but not to himself. Despite these visual and verbal warnings, Maria did smoke from her early teen-age years on. I never did, except a cigar at a special event or when I had a few drinks, or the five or six times I tried marijuana as an adult. My father knew about addictions to gambling and drinking, but could never recognize that smoking is an addiction too. He paid with his life and so did Maria, except she added another devastating addiction, alcohol. Lois's mother Eleanor Davidson Grant died of these same addictions, too. There were millions of others before and after them, too.

When the veterans came home from what was termed The Great War or later on World War I, they were seen as heroes and saviors. After all, they were the defenders of democracy and the victors in the world war that was supposed to end all wars. America and American servicemen were riding high in praise and adoration. My father returned to be with his buddies in downtown Manhattan after staying in France, these were his roots and what he understood best. There was no government program to help the veterans at that time, no educational benefits, no retraining, no loans or home mortgages. None of that was available to veterans until the end of World War II when Congress passed the G.I. Bill, one of the finest pieces of legislation ever. That G.I. Bill provided extensive educational, training and financial benefits for those honorably discharged from the military service. It was paid back ten-fold in the income taxes these individuals paid, as well as providing major numbers of needed well trained and professional personnel throughout the country. This enlightened legislation helped America and its citizens since then and has still benefited us as a society.

At the end of World War I, returning veterans had to depend primarily on local assistance, mostly political in its structure. In New York City, that meant the Democratic Party machine. When you needed help, you went to your local Democratic precinct captain to learn what was available in jobs or schooling, and told him what you were interested in. Somebody in the local political office took notes, made some phone calls, and things got done. No one really asked how it all happened, but it did.

Some veterans wanted to become cops or firemen, others wanted to work for the post office or open a corner newsstand. Unless there was some conflict with another person wanting exactly the same corner or job, you usually got what you asked for. If not, you had to wait for another opening, or choose something else. Of course in return for this favored treatment and assistance, you owed your allegiance to the local party organization for the rest of your life. This translated to consistently without fail supporting the organization's candidates, regardless of their qualifications and commitments, whether you liked them or not, or if they were doing an effective job. Once they were elected, whatever they did was their business, not yours, and you tolerated it. That was the price of admission for getting what you wanted. This devoted format generally worked well for both the returning veterans, the party, and particularly the elected officials.

My father wanted to open a restaurant or cafeteria at the corner of Franklin and Centre Streets in New York City, and the political leaders made it happen. With many people moving to and from the subway lines in the area, this was an ideal spot for a restaurant. Many other buildings were being constructed in the same area, and this meant potential eating customers. He also was given the concession to serve meals to the prisoners and those awaiting trial in the nearby Tombs, which had no kitchen facilities at that time. The political machine took care of the details, helping my father get the necessary permits and even possibly providing some start-up money, where it came from was never mentioned.

For the rest of his life my father was fully committed to the Democratic Party. No matter who the candidates were or for whatever office, he only knew how to pull the voting levers for the Democratic slate. The local machine had helped him have the restaurant he wanted so badly, and that was it. There was never anything as important as loyalty. My father voted the Democratic ticket for the rest of his life, on the local, state and national levels. As far as he was concerned, no other party or candidate ever ran. He deeply believed that the Republicans were only for big business and the rich, and therefore against all others, especially the lower and middle classes.

My father's restaurant at Franklin and Centre Streets turned out to be quite successful; he sometimes bragged that it was the largest cafeteria in Manhattan at the time, though we were never sure. Because of the heavy pedestrian traffic in the area, along with all sorts of municipal and court offices, he did very well.

He was smart enough to know the importance and benefits of getting along with the local precinct police, who were quite powerful at the time, and it seemed the right thing for a decent person to do. My father let the on-duty, local precinct have full access to the restaurant kitchen area. Here they could hide, warm up on cold nights, have coffee and cake, use the toilet and stay out of trouble, maybe even catch some shut eye. This was fine, until one night when several cops began fighting over some probably inconsequential topic, and wrecked a good portion of the kitchen. Worse than this, in the heat of the battle one of them pulled out his gun and fired a round. Fortunately the wayward bullet hit no one, but the sound of the shot helped to end the ongoing skirmish.

Once my father found out about the fight he acted immediately, as he did all his life. He found out who caused the most trouble, the same officer who had fired his gun. Through his now expanding political connections and contacts he'd acquired through the restaurant and the Tombs, he got this aberrant policeman abruptly transferred to godforsaken, dreaded, remote Staten Island. No reasonable person, especially a cop on night tours, ever wanted to go to Staten Island and die of the boredom in that borough. After the officer was there for a short while, he learned how he'd ended up in this swamp-like area. He visited my father and pleaded for his help to get him back to the city and civilization. He told my father the mosquitoes were huge and he had to wear protective netting when he walked his patrol, day or night, and the ferry trip was long and inconvenient from his home. My father listened, and then refused. Because he was the product of the streets of Manhattan, he had learned to be unforgiving in some situations. Because this cop fired his gun in the fight and caused so much trouble, my father had to stop giving kitchen privileges to the police. Because of this cop's stupidity and temper along with my father's intractability, everyone other than my father paid a price. That was the way things went.

By now it's clear that I have many more details and stories about my father than my mother. Why is this? My father had a more complicated and varied life. He came out of the streets and spent a good portion of his life battling, fighting and seeking his perceived rights. He also took part in a wide range of activities, legal and illegal, that brought him near all sorts of characters and experiences. In addition, he told my sister and me many more stories about his life experiences than our mother did. He told his stories in a detailed and exciting way, no matter what the topic he was describing. It never dawned on us that he might be embellishing them or only telling us those portions he wanted us to know.

Whether all of the tales are totally true or not, it's clear that my father's life on the streets of Manhattan, beginning at such a young age, made him a tough, savvy and forever suspicious person. He had a wary edge to him, what you might expect of some animal in the wild. He had at least the equivalent of a baccalaureate in street smarts, maybe even a Ph.D. In many respects he was brighter than some of the educated people I've known, people with official Ph.D.s, MDs and other comprehensive academic qualifications. His street career forced him to learn the importance of making money, of finding ways to survive despite his disadvantages, and gave him the cunning and guile he needed to offset his limited formal education.

Still, he was always aware of his lack of formal education, perhaps even self-conscious, and he spent much time as an adult trying to catch up. At one point he took a public speaking course through a local adult education program. He reported doing well in telling stories there, but never yielding his distinct New York City accent. He always asked questions about things he didn't know about, never hiding what he didn't know. Once when we were driving towards the city on Horace Harding Boulevard in Queens, looking at the Empire State Building and the other buildings in the distant skyline, he suddenly broke the silence and asked me "Buddy, what is physics?" No one had ever asked me that question before or since. As a freshman at Columbia I had some understanding of physics, but this is not an easy question to answer. I tried to make the explanation as clear as I could with the knowledge I had, but I'm not sure I succeeded. Whatever I did say at the time must have satisfied him.

My father talked about knowing Sister Mother Cabrini, a well-respected nun who helped the poor. When they were both young, living on the lower East Side in Manhattan, he sometimes walked and talked with her. Because of this connection he often visited the church named after her, somewhere in either upper Manhattan or the Bronx on Fort Washington Blvd. between Henry Hudson Pkwy and Broadway, just south of Fort Tryon Park. He told us he would kneel and pray and light votive candles before the altar where her preserved body is on display behind a protective glass partition He never told us why he had these one-way conversations.

Some members of my father's family had a successful and unusual business in the so-called rag and twine trade. This title seemed confusing but that was the name of the trade. His sister Tessie and some of her Marrona relatives owned several large flatbed trucks and had contracts to pick up and remove the paper waste from office buildings in Manhattan at night after the offices were closed. After collecting the paper they bound it in huge bundles with bailing wire and took it to certain train yards. From there it was shipped to Canada where it was reprocessed into fresh paper at the paper mills. I think they used the recycled paper to make newsprint and other products.

Apparently the Marrona family was able to take advantage of the paper mill operators' slow payments, and that was fine with them. The family received a premium for every delay, sometimes waiting three to six months or a year for payment. The longer they waited, the greater the premium and profit. My father told us he had a chance to join this business, but felt it was beneath him, and besides, he wanted to be an independent businessman more directly responsible for the outcome. I suspect there were other motivations including personality differences with other family members. I believe that syndicates controlled this rag and twine industry, that's what it was called, and they decided who would work in specific territories. In any case, most of our relatives in this business did extremely well. Each of them had homes in Brooklyn, the Jersey shore, Florida and Canada. When they weren't working, and this was hard work, they would travel to one of their homes for needed rest and relaxation.

Unfortunately, my father and his sister Tessie did not speak for years from right after their mother died. This meant my sister and I never again saw our aunts, uncles, and cousins on Aunt Tessie's side of the family. Apparently the split was over money and valuable possessions, including a beautiful Waltham tri-gold pocket watch belonging to my grandfather. After my grandmother died in 1938, Aunt Tessie became the family matriarch and supposedly told her siblings with some harshness, "From now on, everybody stays in their own house." Apparently my father had asked about their mother's belongings and related items including money that had been left by their mother. When the discussion became heated, he and others were ordered out of the house. My father was easily offended and his hurt lasted virtually the rest of their lives until just before both he and Tessie died. My father and his other sister Carmela remained close for years after and we continued to see them on Sundays, but eventually we lost the connection for no apparent reason. Maybe it was because we'd moved to Queens from Brooklyn and once my father and aunt Carmela died there was little reason anymore. A few years ago I did call my cousin Rocky, spoke with his daughter named Carmela, but he did not want to speak with me directly, even though he was there. He never responded to my message.

My father was deeply hurt by Tessie's order to stay away. He never saw or talked to her or her children again until she visited him at the Veteran's Administration hospital just before he died of cancer. This was a belated and somewhat meaningless reconciliation. Both died of cancer within weeks of the visit. How sad that a brother and sister did not speak to one another for so many years, almost 20 years, until it was really too late. By then they were almost complete strangers. There's no explanation for such familial breaks over what really was a silly dispute. Everyone involved would have done better to resolve the issue long before his or her positions became hardened to irreconcilable memories.

This brother and sister dispute had a strange partial resolution many years later. Maybe ten years after Lois and I had moved to Leonia, somewhere around 1975, an insured package arrived from Florida. It was addressed to me, but we didn't recognize the return address. When I opened the package I found a carefully wrapped present, cushioned with tissue paper. It was my grandfather's beautiful tri-color gold Waltham pocket watch, I recognized it immediately because it had been shown to me as a boy. The enclosed note was signed by two of my first cousins, Pauline and Mary, Aunt Tessie's children, now quite old and permanently living in Florida. The note said they thought that my grandfather's watch rightfully belonged to me. I stared at the massive watch, opening its beautifully decorated front and rear gold case to look at the face and the mechanism. I looked at it for a long time. An object of dispute was being offered to me.

I wrote to my cousins the next day, thanking them for their kindness and expressing my sadness how their mother and my father, a brother and a sister hadn't spoken to one another for so many years because of some poorly defined dispute over possessions. Naturally, I realized there was more to the dispute than a watch, most likely a considerable amount of my grandmother's money. My cousins never replied and I do not know if they are still alive, although at this point I doubt it, they were considerably older than I was.

Years later I had the watch appraised and was surprised to find it is worth more than two thousand dollars. I keep the watch in a safety deposit box at the local bank. Whenever I go there, I take out the watch and think about its history and the disagreement it caused. I have thought about selling it but believe I should pass it on to our children. I have virtually nothing else from my father's side of the family and but a few of his possessions, a metal hip flask, a leather folder to hold removable shirt collars, a Bulova watch, some books of his and some family photographs. After a lifetime, that's a meager collection. There's also a Seth Thomas banjo-style clock hanging in our dining room that chimes on the half hour and hour. I wind it once a week, usually on the same day, and it always makes me think of my father doing this same thing when Maria and I were children. There's one other major item, my parents' beautifully striking dining room chest which I will consider later on.

I sometimes also think of a less pleasant memory still imprinted in my mind. When I was about 7 or 8 my father took me to boxing matches at the Fort Hamilton, an army base in Brooklyn. We'd park outside the base and he'd hold my hand as we walked to the entrance. One summer night as we were going to the base, a large man came down the street, unsteady on his feet. I didn't understand that he was drunk, but my father did. As the man came close he bumped into my father and hit him right in the groin with his swinging arm and hand. My father let go of my hand and bent over in pain. He might have even yelled a bad word (any word children were forbidden to use but which adults used when upset or angry). The other man wheeled around, still unsteady and grabbed my father by his summer shirt and threw him up on the hood of a parked car. His speech was slurred and he called my father a "guinea wop," a term I had never heard.

My father tried to politely reason with the man, telling him he was with his son, how we were going to the fights at the base and he was sorry he had gotten in the way. My father stayed calm and collected while he spoke. Eventually the man let go of my father and he slid off the car to the sidewalk. I'd never seen my father looking vulnerable. He got up, said nothing, took my hand and we went on to the fights. People sitting on the front porches of nearby houses directly on that street witnessed the whole thing, but none of them came to help or even asked what had happened. They couldn't have missed this scene.

When we got home that night my father told my mother we were going to the fights again the next night. This seemed strange because we'd never gone to the fights two nights in a row. Besides, there were fights at Fort Hamilton only once a week. But my mother didn't question him. The next night at about the same time, he parked the car near where the drunken man had hit him. This was a beautiful black, two-door coupe, 1940 Pontiac, with a metal hood ornament of an Indian's head in profile. My father said nothing and I was still confused about the earlier incident. Or maybe I was already conditioned not to ask my father about something when he didn't volunteer an explanation. We waited for what seemed to be a long time, and then we went home.

We did the same thing for perhaps a couple more nights. Finally my father saw whom he was looking for, the man who'd thrown him on the hood of the car. My father reached behind the front seat and picked up a large, black, heavy wooden club with a leather strap on one end. It looked just like the ones the New York police used to carry and twirl as they walked their beat; a cop had probably given it to him. My father looked at me and told me to stand by the car, telling me not to be afraid because daddy knew what he was doing. I did not question his instructions.

As the man approached, my father said: "Remember me? The other night?" The man seemed puzzled. When my father reminded him what had happened, this now sober man must have had a remembrance trace of abusing my smaller father. He blurted out "Oh, you're the little guinea wop from the other night." Even sober this man was still nasty, a committed bigot.

With that my father took the club from behind his back, lunged up at the much bigger man and brought the club down on the middle of the man's shoulders with the force of a seasoned blacksmith swinging a hammer. The club made a dull, solid sound, and the man went down screaming in pain. My father turned, picked me up and placed me in the middle of the front seat of the Pontiac where I would be close to him, touching him. He put the club back behind the seat, and stared directly into my face with his beautiful, intense eyes and said: "Buddy, you remember this. When someone hurts you, you have to hurt them back, maybe not right away, but you have to hurt them back."

Well, here I am more than 65 years later and I still remember this event as if it happened this morning. I have often thought about my father's powerful instantaneous retaliation and his admonition to me. I had to wait until I was an early teenager to find out what the hurtful words "guinea" or "wop" meant. Even today, when I hear it, I cringe and think back on the long ago episode with that drunken man.

It was as frightening to me to see this man lying in pain, as it had been to see this same man curse my father and physically humiliate him. Even as I write this, my mouth gets a little dry and I begin to feel a gnawing feeling in my abdomen. Once again I can feel the "fight or flight mechanism," my body's response to a frightening situation. I wonder if under those same circumstances whether I would have fought or fled from the situation. Abstractly, it could be either way.

Consistently, the same people who watched from their porches the night the man brutalized my father also did nothing the night my father retaliated. No one called the police or asked what was going on. None of them moved from their summer relaxation.

How much did this episode affect me? For many years the club my father used so long ago hung in my bedroom clothes closet. In the past when I was taking clothing from that upstairs closet I sometimes heard the club hitting dully against the closet sidewall. Once in a while I take the club off the hook in the first floor closet where it now hangs, hold it as it's meant to be held and look at the dents and markings on its surface. Each time I do this, I think about that isolated time my father used the club so long ago, striking quickly and forcefully. A few years ago I replaced the old, fraying strap with a new leather bootlace. Recently when our dear friend

Grace Dowling Croft was visiting us from Australia, I told her the story of the club. As if to authenticate the details of the story, I brought the club from the closet to show it to her. She looked at the club and then stared at me without a word. I never knew what she was thinking.

As I grew and became more thoughtful, I understood that you don't need to use a club to "get back" at someone who hurt you. I now know that words can be much more powerful than any physical harm. Words last even longer than any blow on the shoulder. Although words leave no marks or bruises, they hurt the mind and soul.

Genetics and upbringing play strange tricks on all of us. Earlier I mentioned how Maria and my mother were often angry or upset with each other, but gave considerable slack to my father. By contrast, Maria spoke reverently about our father, as if he could walk on water. Maria could tell a story with so much enthusiasm and feeling that she made you believe in her hero.

Maria's adoration of our father might have been why she acted so much like my father, particularly as an adult. Sometimes she seemed to mimic his behavior as if she was his clone. As with my father, you didn't want to cross her. She was tough, yet soft; she could be kind to everybody, yet explosive. She always needed to make her point, and to get even with those who'd hurt her, whether they really had or not. She could dismiss friends who offended her and was unforgiving; if you were subject to her wrath, it could last a long time, maybe forever. Maria had many creative skills and was highly intelligent, yet she seldom seemed to use these qualities for her own positive purposes. For example, in various work positions she held she would try to run a particular organization with her strong will and force others to do what she believed. This was so even if she'd not had leadership responsibilities. It frequently did not work to her favor.

Our father had a keen sense of humor, and he liked to play with Maria and me. Some people might have thought he was being silly, but we saw no silliness; we loved the games he created. For many years we'd go to Times Square on New Year's Day, the morning after the boisterous New Year's Eve celebration there. He told us we were going there to look for the money somehow left behind by the celebrants before the Department of Sanitation quickly cleaned up the streets. Maria and I would walk on the edge of the sidewalks carefully searching for any coins or bills that someone had accidentally dropped. We'd move through the papers and litter, seeking our fortune.

It took us years to realize that our father had been moving ahead of us, quietly dropping change along the pavement while under the guise of also looking with us. We never suspected anything. Whenever one of us would "discover" coins, we'd be surprised and pleased. Later on, after we counted our bounty, we'd have breakfast at a Horn and Hardart's Automat, a famous chain of cafeterias that had good and cheap food and drinks behind individual glass doors that you opened by inserting coins. We loved this annual adventure and couldn't wait to get home and tell our mother about our success. I'm sure our mother was in on the joke, but she never told us, she just smiled.

We almost always ate our evening meal as a family, something my mother thought was an important way for us to be together and talk and review our daily activities. My father usually had a glass or two of red wine with dinner, sometimes adding ice and cream soda and might give us a sip or two. After having his wine, dad would sometimes tell us he'd had too much to drink and he'd feign falling asleep, putting his head down, pretending to snore. He might even mumble that he was "drunk," though he'd just been totally coherent and sober. I guess we never figured out that he was acting. But once he made this announcement and gone through his routine, which we got to expect, Maria and I took it as an open invitation to put our arms around his neck and reach carefully into his trouser pocket, taking as much of his folded money as we could, trying not to wake him with our excited glee and laughter at supposedly being adroit pickpockets. We always succeeded and didn't understand why.

We then ran into the living room where we'd sit and count our loot. Then my father would make a sudden recovery from sleeping and drinking, yelling out to our mother that he'd been robbed and demanding to know who could have done this, and how he thought he was safe in our home. Once in a while he'd tell her to call the police. Meanwhile, Maria and I would be giggling, maybe a bit frightened he would actually do this. When my father came into the living room he'd ask us if we knew what happened to his money or if we saw someone take it. We'd try to remain calm and expressionless, a difficult task for two young children, then we'd either laughingly confess and return the money, or would pretend to lie until we were laughing so hard he would "uncover" the full truth. As we got older we outgrew this game, and recognized its phases, but it is still a strong memory.

I never understood why my father played these games that let us believe we had found money in the streets or that we'd actually stolen his money. I never heard about anyone else's father doing this. Was he trying to convey some hidden meaning? Did he recognize any possible repercussions once we discovered that these games were essentially hoaxes? Did he want us to learn some lesson about the transience of money? If there was a reason, he kept it to himself.

My father also had an amusing game involving traffic lights that took us years to get wise to. We were always driving somewhere, visiting relatives, going upstate, heading to local parks or traveling through the boroughs. Our father convinced us he could make a traffic light change from red to green just by saying: "Change. Frank Muzio and his family are coming up to the light, we do not want to be delayed by a red light, so go green, please, and do it now." Maria and I would watch intensely and sure enough the light magically changed to green without my father even slowing down or speeding up. He could make this happen light after light through a number of blocks. The more he did it, the more we laughed and the more our parents smiled. We had such strong unyielding faith in our father's powers and never figured out for years how his voice could change the signal lights.

My father revealed to us many years later that he had no unusual powers. Back in those days, he said, the traffic lights did not have side covers or shields, so he could see them from their sides as they cycled from green to amber to red, or just green to red with no in between amber arrangement and he could consistently tell when they were going to change.

One special event I remember took place one summer when I was about 5 and my cousin Eugene Stramiello was about 10. Both our families were in Saratoga Springs, New York for the summer horseracing season, where my father was a legal bookmaker. The racing season was several weeks longer than it is now. Eugene and I were playing near a large fenced area that looked as if it held thousands of chickens, a huge army of birds cackling, constantly moving about, busily pecking the ground.

I don't remember why we were at this farm but what happened next is still crystal clear. Somehow, Eugene and I wandered away from our parents and figured out how to open the gate to this massive chicken pen. Once we unhooked the gate and opened the entranceway it was as if we'd granted the chickens some special dispensation, and they immediately ran out of the pen, randomly smacking into one another in their frenetic escape route. We could only stand back and watch while hundreds, maybe thousands of chickens stampeded past into the nearby open fields. We were scared as only a child can be, and, though we must have realized the full magnitude of what we had done, we had no idea how to correct it, to return it to the way it had been before our aberrant action.

Luckily, my father always knew how to make matters right. When he suddenly arrived and saw the chicken chaos and realized the foolish thing Eugene and I had done, he didn't reprimand us but took action. He went and found the farmer who owned the chickens and soon the farmer, his workers and even Eugene and I began chasing and rounding up the escaped chickens. I'm pretty sure we got most of the chickens, though probably not all of them. To make things better, my father offered the farmer some money, probably a lot of money. My father was upset but also patiently understood that we had merely been acting like foolish children. Whenever anyone retold this story, the one uncertainty was how many chickens escaped. My father insisted it was a couple of thousand, but he might have been exaggerating. He often did.

Even so, only someone who has done it or something comparable can fully know the sheer terror of being a five-year-old who has let a couple thousand, even a couple hundred noisy chickens escape their bordered location. The thought of it still remains fresh 70 years after it happened, although now I see it just as innocent child's play.

On Easter Sundays, we'd get all dressed up and our parents would take us to Fifth Avenue for the Easter Parade, followed by dinner in a nice restaurant, though our celebration had nothing to do with any religious significance of Easter. Sometimes we ate at the Turf Restaurant or one of the many Italian restaurants in the city, and sometimes at the Scandinavian House. When we first went to the Scandinavian House, I didn't understand how to eat what was called "smorgasbord style," where food of all sorts was piled high on a massive central serving table and attractively presented. You would walk around this table and pick out what you wanted, anything displayed. Since no one explained that you could go back as often as you wanted or that the food was organized into various courses, I did not notice that my parents ate in an orderly pattern, first appetizers and then other dishes in sequence. I just mixed everything up, so my herring was mixed with my dessert and other seafood items mingled with the fruit, all piled on my plate. It didn't look too attractive. By the next time we went there, I had figured it out. Nobody told me there was a more orderly culinary way to do this; it was one of those discovery processes my parents let take place in our experiences.

Sometimes, we ate at Jack Dempsey's Restaurant on the west side of Broadway, I think around West 48th or West 49th Street. Mr. Dempsey, a former heavyweight champion of the world, was often in the restaurant, usually near the front, wearing a nice suit. He looked huge. My father would take me over to shake his hand and I remember my hand being buried in Mr. Dempsey's massive hand. When he looked down at me, he made me somehow think he liked me, he'd smile, but of course he didn't even know me. When I compare pictures of the younger Jack Dempsey with photos of my father at a comparable age, I see a resemblance, though, of course, my father was significantly smaller and never heavyweight champion of the world.

Dempsey was called the "Manassas Mauler," and my father had gone to several of his championship fights with some of his buddies, including his brother-in-law Joe Strike, another gambler. My father loved Jack Dempsey and usually bet large amounts of money on him to win.

Dempsey had lost to Gene Tunney twice, including the famous "long count" bout, in which Tunney had additional time to recover from a knockdown by Dempsey. My father never believed that Tunney won legitimately. He undoubtedly was biased because he liked Dempsey and must have bet heavily on him to win, so he lost. But my father always respected how Dempsey never complained and never blamed anybody for what happened. The lesson to me was, "When you lose, say little; when you win, say less." Eventually, Dempsey and Tunney became lifelong friends, and by retiring relatively young they avoided especially the mental scars of becoming what former boxers were frequently referred to as "punch drunk," a vividly accurate term describing their significant loss of capacities.

As I was growing up, my father would take me to hang out with some of his friends. One of these was named Patsy, and he looked like an ex-prizefighter. He had scar tissue over his eyes, and his nose was pushed in and bent in several places. One of his ears was bent over too. He also talked with some difficulty, though probably he too was what they called "punch drunk" after all his fights. But he was always friendly to me and always talked with me about school and sports, even though his words were unclear. My father, Patsy and I would rent a rowboat in Brooklyn and go crabbing. They did most of the rowing, though I sometimes helped with one oar while one of them handled the other. After we dropped the baited crab traps overboard, we waited for a while and drifted. In the meantime, they would talk, I would listen, and then we'd dig into the huge hero sandwiches Patsy had bought for the trip. When we brought up the traps, they often contained a couple of crabs. At the end of the day, we'd share the crabs equally with Patsy. We brought ours for my mother to add to her famous Italian red sauce. After a full meal, I would try to fall asleep, but it took me hours. Every time I'd start to doze off, I felt that I was still rocking in the boat drifting on the water. It took a long time before precious sleep came. Sometimes I imagined I was "seasick," but wasn't sure what this was.

I've already told you how my father could sometimes be explosive, but thank goodness these occasions were rare. I once tried to follow his example. When I was a hormonally exploding teenager I got into a brief conflict with him, probably over some insignificant long forgotten matter. I suddenly put up my hands in a boxer's stance. My father suggested I didn't want to do that, but I thought I did. After all, I had recently completed a combative boxing course at Columbia with Professor Paul Governali as my instructor. From my instructed stance armed with my newly acquired combative knowledge, I foolishly and aggressively lunged, swinging at my father with a quick left-hand jab. He quickly blocked me with his right forearm and with a partially closed fist punched me right on the jaw with a sharp left hand blow, knocking me to the floor. I was shocked. Nothing like this had ever happened to me before. This wasn't like being tackled in football or being tagged by a fielder's glove in the face when sliding into a base. I really did see those stars sometimes described by others. My father quickly reached down, pulled me up even though I was bigger than he was and hugged me. He even showed me how I'd "telegraphed" or visibly gave away what punch I was intending to throw at him. Once again he was serving as my teacher. It was the only time I ever did something so stupidly aggressive. I think he could have knocked me out if he'd hit me with full force of his powerful shoulder and fist.

Louie Gillette, another good friend of my father's, owned a Gulf gas station on Queens Boulevard, towards Long Island City, where we sometimes visited him. Louie was a bulky, muscular man with a broad, open face. He smiled a lot and seemed to get along with everybody. For many years he had been a coalminer in Wilkes-Barre or Hazleton, Pennsylvania. I'm not sure how he and my father became friends. When we visited him, my father got some gas, and then we'd sit around and talk – I mostly listened – as the men had coffee and I drank a soda.

One time Louie told us what it was like to work in the coalmines, something I guess he didn't miss. His description confirmed this. He told us that one of the few safety devices the miners had was a cage of chirping canaries they brought into the mine. They kept the canaries nearby when they worked in the dark excavating tunnels. If the canaries stopped singing it was a warning that the air had turned bad for these small creatures and the miners would quickly sometimes chaotically leave the mine. Louie stopped being a miner during World War II when he joined the Navy, and never returned. Running a gas station had certain drawbacks, but it was far better than mucking coal in dangerous and oxygen-depleted caves deep below the earth's surface.

One day my father and I were in the dirty, ill-kempt office at Louie's gas station when another incident caught me totally off guard. My father was dressed up that day and had on a new pair of shoes, probably one of his custom-made ones. One of the other men in the office, someone we didn't know, twice stepped on my father's shoe, scuffing it. The first time might have been accidental but the second was clearly but inexplicably deliberate. My father stood in front of the man who had marred his shiny shoes, looked up at him and without a word, stomped right on the man's foot. When the man bent over in pain my father hit him in the jaw and knocked him to the ground. For a minute or so, this guy was out cold.

Louie came in from pumping gas and asked what had happened when he saw this man slowly recovering. When my father told his version, Louie accepted it; he knew my father wouldn't make up a story. He then helped the man off the floor and the incident was over. Once again, I had seen my father's belief in swift justice. In many ways his reaction and fierce physical response were beyond order and civility, but that didn't change what he had done. None of us can ever forget his climb out of the lower East Side of Manhattan.

My father's street experience also taught him that if a dollar could be made, he would find a way to do it, legally if possible, but sometimes not so legally or even downright illegally. He was never again going to let deprivation and disadvantage rule his life or his family's. If he wanted to get something done, he didn't want anyone to get in the way of achieving his goal. Sometimes he used politeness and sweet-talk; other times he used money, a bribe or an inducer. He always felt that a drop of honey worked better than a bucket of vinegar and believed that every person has his price. This price wasn't necessarily money, but something the person wanted or needed, some other kind of benefit. My father was able to find out what made someone tick and then used that knowledge to get the person to do what my father wanted. I learned and used some of these skills as a teenager and even once or twice as a Marine Corps officer.

My father stayed connected to the local Democratic Party and its leaders, and this served him well over the years. He knew Al Smith, who was elected four times as Governor of New York, and who eventually ran for president. He knew Jimmy Walker, the infamous Mayor of New York, and his powerful district leaders. These connections paid off when the Great Depression hit in 1929. Businesses closed, people lost their jobs and few people could afford to eat at restaurants. Despite its long success, my father eventually had to close his restaurant at Franklin and Centre Streets. The restaurant had already lost business after the city connected two subway lines by tunnel, reducing the number of pedestrians passing by the restaurant and eating there. People stopped eating out when they have no jobs or money.

My father later told me that about the time Maria was born on January 29, 1930, shortly after the beginning onslaught of the Great Depression and a few years into my parents' marriage, he had exactly $13.55 in his pocket, along with many unpaid bills. The Great Depression hit everybody and lasted well into 1941, when the United States entered the war against Germany, Italy and Japan and began a massive, war economy with high employment, military service and intense defense production. World War II created a boom economy and a totally new focus for America and its people.

In 1929-1930, my father was 38 or 39, broke economically, and somewhat broken in spirit, like millions of other Americans. But, with his energy and resilience, he somehow arranged through his connections to the New York Democratic Party to become one of the bookmakers authorized to take bets at major horseracing tracks on the East Coast from Saratoga to Florida. At the time, before states began controlling betting directly, private bookmakers acted as independent operators under loose state supervision. Each bookmaker paid a fee to gain an assigned location at each track, and booked bets as a private contractor. Most of the bookmakers had a certain following of bettors. My dad took bets in the upper grandstand, near the finish line, that was his spot at the various tracks. This was an ideal location because the horseplayers liked to congregate there, where they had a birds-eye view of the ending portion of every race. It was a premier location and a premier life for the bookmaker and for his family too.

From our early childhood, my father always reminded my sister and me that the only person who consistently wins is the bookmaker. There were no exceptions. Sure, some characters at the racetrack, including some of his best customers, constantly tried to perfect their systems to "beat the ponies," why they even won once in a while, partially confirming their supposed skills. Some of these sure-thing systems were based on superstitions, others on mathematical formulas, sometimes even the calculations by supposedly sound rational Harvard graduates. Some depended on tips from jockeys, trainers, horse owners, maybe a neighbor who knew someone working at the track. But of course none of these schemes worked. These addicted, self-deceived gamblers might win for a short period, a couple of races in a row, a few days longer. But over time, they all lost, always. They somehow always remembered the times they won, would describe the specific races this happened, and were ahead with glee, but they had total amnesia about all times they'd lost again and again, before and after. Even young losing gamblers acted like Alzheimer's patients. Some were so sure they would win again that they'd pawn their wife's jewelry or even steal or borrow from their employers. Their commitment to their gambling addiction had the utmost thoughtless priority over any rationale and it inevitably ruined their lives, their marriages and careers; sometimes they became so helpless, shattered and devastatingly lost they took their own lives because of the self-inflicted messes they created on their whims. This was hardly the "Sport of Kings," rather it was just the "Sport of Chumps and Losers."

Many others foolishly sought a combination of solace and capital from loan sharks who provided them with cash at extremely high rates of interest that were compounded until the loan was paid back. Most compulsive gamblers deluded themselves into believing they would eventually have a major "killing" or win so much that all of their debts would be offset. Then, their lives would become gloriously, magically successful. Naturally, that never happened. Loan sharks are unforgiving. They are cold, calculating, sometimes brutal, and could never let someone welch on them. They always got their money and/or their pound of flesh, or more. Everyone knew what the outcome would be; yet time and again compulsive gamblers went in desperation to loan sharks.

Paradoxically, although my father was deeply embedded in the gambling culture, he was immune to its temptations.

Because the bookmakers always won, our lives were comfortable, no, more than just comfortable by most people's standards. We had attractive apartments, always had a nice up-to-date car, traveled well, went on vacations and had plenty of money. My father sometimes kept unusually large amounts of cash around for short periods of time, though we never knew where it went. Once while we were living in Bay Ridge, when we were 10 and 8, my sister and I counted $80,000 in cash. My father found it amusing because it took us a long time to count as we stacked the money in denominational piles at the kitchen table. Our hands especially our fingertips were filthy dirty from all the counting and they even smelled funny. We had to wash them thoroughly afterwards.

Unfortunately, what had been legal and accepted was about to become legislatively illegal. Somehow, the political powers came up with a new system of betting, at least new to the United States, a system used in England and France, called pari-mutuels. A man in France invented the system around 1877 and called it the "Paris mutuels," eventually shortened to "pari-mutuels." This term, which means "amongst us," was a method of determining betting odds by the amounts of money bet win, place and show (first, second, third, respectively), with the house taking a commission from the total pool. In other words, gamblers are betting against each other, not the house or a bookmaker's calculations. Starting around 1940, various states adopted pari-mutuel betting, thereby taking direct control of betting. This meant that the states, through their structured racing commissions, became the state's bookmakers, bringing in more money directly for the state and also providing wider political patronage to those in power and their supporters for the more bureaucratic and concentration operations.

Once the states took over, what would happen to my father and all the other bookmakers who'd been operating legally for all these years? (By this time my father had been a legal bookmaker for about 10 years.) It would have been reasonable and in many respects economically sound to include these bookmakers in the new system. After all, they were successful businessmen who knew about betting at racetracks and had a history of doing a sound job.

What did happen, according to my father, was that state officials invited the bookmakers to a special meeting, telling them beforehand their views would be given full and open discussion. But, instead the officials politely told the bookmakers their working days at the racetracks were over. The state would not hire them but would give the jobs to newly trained, politically connected people. At the meeting Pinkerton Security officials took the former bookmakers' pictures and not so politely told them to stay away from the racetracks. They'd been fired, put out of business. My father said the warning was quite clear: Come around the tracks and you'll be removed, maybe beaten up. From then on and abruptly, bookmakers were enemies of the state, forbidden to practice their livelihood. These suddenly unemployed and humiliated bookmakers were hardly stupid or unimaginative men. They were excellent thinkers who had many abilities; they knew about profits and losses and understood statistics and probability. So these removed bookmakers banded together and quickly formed bookmaking syndicates, albeit illegal ones that were located away from the racetracks. Some of them, although not my father, decided to test the

Pinkerton threats and continued to conduct bookmaking at racetracks where they could be near the owners, trainers, jockeys, stable workers, and others who wanted an alternative to the mutuel windows, and maybe better odds. Bookmakers also let bettors run a tab when placing a bet.

Later on in my life, I learned that my father had once loaned about $35,000 to a man opening a bowling alley in Long Island City, charging a high rate of interest. When the man failed to pay the loan plus the growing interest, he fled to Florida. As soon as my father found out, I heard him on the phone talking to one of his friends in Florida, Joe Peters. I don't remember whether my father just described the possibly fleeing man or told Joe what train he'd taken and could be expected in Florida. And I don't know if my father told Joe what to do, but he did not return to Long Island City. After a while his bowling alley was put on the market. I don't know what happened and I don't know if my father ever got his money back; I never asked. I remembered his standard answer, almost his mantra was: "Don't ask no questions."

While moving into becoming a successful off-the-track bookmaker and occasional loan shark, my father also returned to his original enterprise and earlier interest, owning and running restaurants. He used to call himself as a "restaurateur." He was good at investigating and analyzing data on such matters, just as he was in helping me to select a college. He'd identify locations with good potential, including studying walking and driving patterns in the restaurant's proximal area, then buying one that was run-down and building it into a newer, more modern, well-appointed restaurant or diner. Once it was successful for a reasonable time, he'd profit from the sale of the business and move on to another challenging project.

Later on, once I found out about his bookmaking involvement, it also became patently clear what the advantages my father had by running a local restaurant business. This duality of a restaurant/bookmaking site created a fine venue for providing reasonable and sound cover for his illegal bookmaking operations. There's frequent daily traffic in and out of restaurants; within large populations of dining customers there are segments that want to conveniently place bets; and the two enterprises matched perfectly.

He often came home in the afternoon after working hard in one of his restaurants. He would strip off the food-stained, sweaty white pants and shirt he wore in the restaurant, take a shower and then take a nap. When he awoke, he'd put on a clean, starched uniform, and be ready for the rest of the day.

As I've said, my father was particular about his clothes. He loved to shop at some of the most exclusive stores in New York City and Miami Beach. When he was younger he had his suits made to order and had shoes custom-made too. He told us he had some sort of unusual body, a "hollowed back," or indentation he once showed me, he had to have his suits and sports jackets made for his physique so they would fit properly, perfectly by his standards. He hated off-the-rack suit jackets whose fabric bunched up and bulged on the back and neck. Along with well-fitting suits, he liked to wear colorful bowties, the kind you have to tie each time. No ready-made, clip-on bowties for Frank Muzio: they were phony, didn't look good, and that was the lazy, quick way. On more casual occasions he'd wear a long-sleeved sports shirt (to hide the now undesired tattoos on his arms), open at the collar, with a matching or contrasting ascot. Here was a man with a sixth grade education, right off the Manhattan streets, looking like some English gentleman on his estate. A sports commentator would have said, "He was playing within himself," an expression that describes a player who moves smoothly and efficiently, but without flamboyance or bravado.

When he did wear ready-made clothes he often went to Sulka's, which I think was on Park Avenue. Sulka's had a store in Paris beginning in 1904, and perhaps my father became familiar with it then when he was there after World War I. One time he walked into Sulka's in Manhattan on his way back to the restaurant wearing one of his clean, crisp white uniforms and white shoes. He wandered around the store but all the salesmen ignored him because of the way he was dressed. It was obvious he didn't fit the image of a well-heeled upper class Sulka's customer. My father could never tolerate discrimination toward himself or others, and after a while, he asked to see the store manager. I wish I had been there when he confronted the manager to demand why he was treated so poorly because of his white uniform. He was a good customer, he had money and he expected to be treated like everyone else who entered that store. From then on those salesmen knew him and gave him the attention he wanted, even if perhaps begrudgingly.

My father's consistent ability to solve problems was one of the reasons I got into Columbia in 1950 as a member of the bicentennial class. My mother had virtually nothing to say about my educational plans; maybe she thought I knew what I was doing. But my father was always able to find answers and influence my life. When I was preparing to go to college he took me to visit several schools on the East Coast, mostly in New York State. For reasons I still don't understand, I was reluctant to go to college too far away.

With these trips, my father did so much more for me than I ever did for any of our three sons. I do not understand why I did not take our sons to the colleges they might be interested in, though most parents automatically do this these days. Because we are both college professors, Lois and I certainly know a great deal about colleges, positive and negative. But each of our sons made this critical decision with little assistance from us. Of course there were high school guidance counselors, and we passively yielded to their advice. In retrospect, this might not have been such a wise approach. After all, why should we have relied on people less qualified than we are to guide our sons' decisions? Our approach contributed to some ambiguity in their selections, along with perplexing academic outcomes.

When we visited colleges, dad had a unique, straightforward, and refreshing approach. He was not interested in visiting with any trained admissions personnel, members of the school's administration, or deans. Nor did he trust the catalogues or any written materials used to recruit students. Instead, he would look students walking around the campuses directly in the eye and ask them about the college. Did they like it there? How are the teachers? (He didn't call them professors.) Was there a lot of drinking going on? What did you do if you were having a problem with a course or a teacher? To him, these students were the most accurate sources, the ultimate consumers. Then we'd walk around to look at the dormitories. He was like some sort of safety inspector, checking the toilets, looking at the fire safety equipment and other features of the buildings. I definitely would have preferred for him not to use his methods. I was uncomfortable with his pronounced New York accent, his occasional misuse of English, and his probing techniques.

Even without a formal education he was comfortable moving about a formal educational setting with the same techniques he used on the streets of Manhattan, or the ways he conducted his restaurant seeking activities. I must have been embarrassed by his directness and inquisitiveness, but at 17, what did I know? His flaws seemed bigger in this formal academic setting, where everybody spoke well and looked good, but how would I have done it? Besides, in his own ways, he found out a great deal of information about each college we visited. He might not have known much about college education, but he did know how to gather information and get a feel for that school. After we left each college, we'd drive away and talk frankly and thoroughly about the experience while it was fresh. Sometimes my conclusions were similar to his, other times I didn't agree.

Eventually I overcame my adolescent procrastination and narrowed down my choices to three New York schools: Cornell University in Ithaca, St. Lawrence University in Canton, and Columbia. I prepared my own applications; my typing skills helped to ease the process. Besides, those were not the days when parents or school advisors helped out, and my parents knew virtually nothing about the application process, or what was rumbling around in my mind. Once again, I was exclusively on my own.

My parents did know that if I attended college, I would be the first one in our extended family. My parents believed it was my burden to do this. As I awaited replies from the schools, my father and mother told me the decision was fully mine. I was having a great deal of trouble deciding whether to go away or stay close to home. At the time I was dating a young woman and feared that I would lose her if I moved away, whatever this meant. Since it had taken me almost two and a half years to finally ask Jeanette Dunphy out, we'd been dating only a few months, and I knew she was taking a job in the city, not going on to college. I never realized I didn't have her or own her, and it took me a while to yield such childish thoughts. Only in primitive slavery or other barbaric relationship can a person own another person.

When the Columbia acceptance letter arrived I was shocked; I didn't think I was worthy. I couldn't make up my mind, and it was causing all sorts of family disruption. A huge packed steamer trunk sat on the living room floor for days, and with each passing day I would vacillate between Columbia, and St. Lawrence, and then back again. It was almost time to leave. I finally asked my father what he would do. After reminding me he wasn't me, he encouraged me to go to Columbia. He didn't know anything about college courses, school reputations or what the Ivy League was, but he had an almost innate respect for Columbia, the way it seemed to fit into the upper West Side integral but separate from the Manhattan pulses. After much procrastination, I took his advice.

I had lunch recently up at Columbia with Bob Wilson, my friend of many years, and my son Edward who'd joined us on a crystal clear late summer day. As we watched the incoming students moving into apartments and dorms I remembered how just 57 years ago I kissed my parents goodbye, took the train and went to Columbia. I got off at the wrong stop, the wrong West 116th Street, but an older man gave me directions and I climbed the many steps of Morningside Park up to Morningside Heights and the university, carrying my two pieces of luggage. On this hot, Indian summer day, I was wearing the suit and tie my father had bought me for my sister Maria's June wedding that year. I was both nervous and awe-struck about entering those halls of ivy; nobody in our family had ever gone to college before, ever. Eventually I found the welcoming and registration building, signed some documents and was given a Columbia blue freshman beanie marked "1954" on its front. I think I wore this cap once or twice to meetings where we learned to sing various Columbia songs. I was now in college.

Unlike me back then, today's students arrived in caravans of Range Rovers and Volvo station wagons, Lexus SUVs, U-Haul trucks, moving vans. And their sweating parents looked like struggling porters hauling the students' microwaves, TVs, DVDs, refrigerators, computers, furnishings, all sorts of personal belongings and supportive paraphernalia. It all seemed so intensely and collectively operational, almost as if some sort of military invasion or preparatory exercise were underway.

I thought how much things had changed in 57 years. I recalled the bare dormitory room on the third floor of Livingston Hall, meeting and feeling awkward about my new roommates, Ralph Mattson from Lead, South Dakota, and Mike Durovich from South River, New Jersey. I had never been away from family and my home other than my stays at Mrs. Stuyver's camp and a few overnight camping trips with the Boy Scouts, not counting those involving my aunts in Brooklyn. The so-called "suite" we shared consisted of two small rooms with bare walls and stark, dark wooden dressers and desks; the common toilets and showers were far down the hall. There was soot on windowsills and there was constant traffic noise on Amsterdam Avenue except late at night. We had no refrigerator, microwave, television sets, not even curtains on the windows. Yessiree, life seemed so much simpler and less cluttered in those days.

All through my time at Columbia, I couldn't believe I was attending an Ivy League school. I was even playing freshman football. I'd never played in high school because there was no team at Long Island City high and my only football experience with a well trained semi-pro team called the Sunnyside Robins, a local club that won a number of championships in Queens. Many of these home games were in Elmhurst Queens and sometimes hundreds of fans for both teams showed up on the sidelines. That was a wonderfully close time with many of my childhood buddies, we used to dress for the games in one player's basement and play college marching songs as we did. We even had a team physician, classy Kelly green and white uniforms, and football plays from a couple of college and professional teams. My father came to a number of the games, but my mother disliked football immensely and never did. She was frequently anticipating some serious, debilitating injury that just never happened. Once or twice my sister Maria and her then boyfriend, Bernie Russell showed up too.

In addition, I think only about 18 out of 234 of my fellow high school graduates went to college. The rest went to humdrum jobs at Eagle Electric, Mojud Hosiery, Louis Sherry Ice Cream and other nearby companies. These others were all fine individuals capable of attending some college, but maybe they were just not aware of opportunities beyond Long Island City and Astoria, or were inhibited by other factors. Many of their parents did not encourage them to attend college, considering it an unneeded luxury. This was especially true for the female students. The part-time guidance counselors offered little counseling and minimal guidance. As with my mother many years before, there were plenty of solid employment opportunities resulting from the burgeoning post World War II economy, so why bother with more education? The goals were similar to my mother's time, get a job, meet someone, get married, have some babies.

But there I was at 18 or 19 enjoying my college days; I was about to be transformed. I wore a dark blue blazer with a light blue Columbia "C" on the breast pocket, had the "Columbia" sticker on the rear window of dad's car, and another letter "C" on the leather luggage I used to carry clothes and books back and forth to college. I also wore a red-striped tie to contrast with the blazer, and whipcord gray flannel slacks with smooth leather piping on the front pockets. I bought these at a store on Broadway and 112th Street that catered to the better dressed Columbia students and professors. (It's still a clothing store there.) I had never spent so much on a pair of trousers before, but they seemed sturdy and well made. They lasted for a long time. I was the essence of Joe Muzio a la Joe College, playing a new role. If you didn't know me, you might think I was an Ivy League student from some formidable prep school in New England, not some kid from the local parochial and New York City Public School systems in Brooklyn and Flushing. According to Alfred Lubrano, in his book, *Limbo*, I was moving from my blue-collar roots to an aspiring white-collar existence where my dreams would become reality.

Years later my friend and now a former colleague, Loretta Brancaccio Taras, with whom I worked at Kingsborough Community College, would sometimes kid me about being someone supposedly with one foot in the Ivy League and the other one in Bay Ridge, Brooklyn. I was one of what Alfred Lubrano in his book *Limbo* also referred to as a "straddler" in two distinct societies. I think I have a better understanding of the blue-collar world I came from than I do of the white-collar world I eventually joined. For most of my college years and adult life I was uncomfortable in situations that drew on what I believed are rigid unspoken white-collar values and beliefs. Now, I have a clearer understanding of at least some of the forces involved in this. Lois once said it would be interesting to study some people with white-collar roots who had achieved blue-collar dreams, the exact reverse of Lubrano's writing.

In late 1950 or early 1951, when I was a freshman or sophomore I accidentally learned that my father was concomitantly a "restaurateur" as well as a bookmaker and loan shark. In my mind up until then, he was only a restaurant owner. On one of my visits home my father, in a moment of confessional revelation, announced that he was a full-fledged member of an organized gambling syndicate. Until then I had no idea. I believed he made his living by owning and managing a series of restaurants and, at one time, a hotel in Roscoe, New York. I'd been at those restaurants and the hotel and even helped at one of them on Jackson Avenue in Long Island City, "The Wheel Food Shoppe," which was smack in the middle of the booming war related factories during the 1940s. I sometimes took my friends to those same restaurants for a meal or snack, when my dad would welcome them and offer them treats. As a young child I took care of the rowboats at the upstate hotel, causing my mother to worry that I would fall in and drown as I nimbly hopped from one boat or brought in a boat that had drifted away from the dock because a guest forgot to tie it properly.

When I arrived that day at our house in Flushing, my father was in the living room, sitting in front of the black and white television set. I leaned over and kissed him, which I did right up until his death, and glanced over at the television screen. I noticed that it showed a pair of well-manicured hands along with the ends of his suit sleeves partially covering a French-cuffed shirt. I asked why the picture showed only the man's hands. My father told me those were hands of a Mr. Frank Costello and Costello was testifying at a hearing before a U.S. Senate committee and didn't want to show his face. He was trying to remain unknown, unrecognizable, but as matters unfolded, that would turn out to be impossible.

The hearings were part of the ongoing investigation into the depth and breadth of organized crime in interstate commerce. Costello was the head of one of the five mob families in New York City, and the government was trying to deport him to Italy, his birthplace. The lead senator was the democrat Estes Kefauver from Tennessee; and the chief counsel was Rudolph Halley. When Costello answered their questions, his voice was hoarse and raspy. You could see the full faces and bodies of the committee members and the audience, but only Costello's hands.

Costello sometimes refused to answer, citing his Fifth Amendment right against self-incrimination. Sometimes he would answer only after pausing to check with his attorney, after the microphones in front of him were covered with his hand or the attorney's. Suddenly, my father blurted out, "Kefauver wants to be President and Halley wants to be the Mayor of New York." He then said angrily, "In the final analysis, they will get nothing, none of them."

When I asked my father to explain this terribly unusual comment, he stared at me and said coldly, "My boy, you just don't get it. Powerful forces control whatever takes place in this country. It isn't the way you think. In order to run for office, you have to make deals, a lot of them; you need big backers who finance your campaign, and once they give you money, you owe them, big time. The money was given in advance of favors that would be asked for and granted. Jobs and influences are controlled the same way. Judgeships are bought, the police are bought, when you want something done, you pay for it. Elected officials are bought every day. Powerful and inner circles controlling money orchestrate it all. If these people think they'll deport Mr. Costello, they're kidding themselves, it will never happen, he's too powerful and they all owe him. They know him and he knows them. And if they think they can convict him and put him in jail, that's even less possible."

I was shocked. Here I was deeply immersed in my freshman courses in Contemporary Civilization and the Humanities. We were reading the works of great thinkers, studying Plato, Aristotle's *Politics*, Rousseau, Durkheim, John Stuart Mills *On Liberty*, Edmund Burke and De Tocqueville's *Democracy in America*, along with many other great writers. My mind was being opened to all sorts of new ideas and perspectives. I had been in a different, totally new world at Columbia, an unknown and exciting territory. I was learning that any qualified citizen could run for and become the president or a mayor, or anything else, and now my father was confronting me with his reality.

How could he say these things? What did he know? How could he be so sure? His words overwhelmed me.

This was how I found out my father was part of an illegal bookmaking syndicate. Once the states started its pari-mutuel gambling system and eliminated bookmaking at the tracks, the bookmakers did what they knew best and formed syndicates to take bets. In their thinking, what difference did it make where you bet?

Under this well-controlled syndicate, my father sometimes ran bookmaking operations in his restaurants and diners that I mentioned earlier. Other times, he had a specific gambling territory, primarily in Greenpoint, Brooklyn and parts of Long Island City. This group had telephone lines and runners to carry bets and money between the bookmakers and their many customers. They also had public officials on their payroll, especially local police officers and their superiors who would ignore what was going on. The cops gambled, too. Everybody justified their involvement in these betting operations, even though they were completely illegal. This was a pervasive, highly organized, corrupt gambling empire controlled by various families who also were engaged in many other activities, and my father was a part of it.

Incidentally, Costello never was deported and continued in his major illegal and legal enterprises. Costello walked out of the hearings after repeatedly refusing to answer questions, and he was never indicted or convicted for any criminal behavior. Like so many other controversial matters, this one died a natural death accompanied by public amnesia. The former flamboyant Mayor of New York, Jimmy Walker, whom my father knew, once said: "The public has a two-week memory." Estes Kefauver made a feeble attempt to run for president and failed; Rudolph Halley might have considered running for Mayor of New York City, but that went nowhere. Later on, Mr. Costello died. Once again, my father was correct.

My father's admissions about his bookmaking career shocked me. I found this all hard to swallow, but I had no control over his life. Eventually, the reality blended into the background as he continued to run his restaurants and his bookmaking endeavors. In turn, I focused on my education, playing sports, and learning how to date college women wearing long, full skirts, attractive matching wool sweaters and brown and white saddle shoes. I closed my mind to his enterprises, although this closure never had any effect on my love and commitments to him and my mother. I never discussed my father's duality with anybody and buried it in my memory. It was the same kind of mental burial I gave to the earlier matter of my cousin Eugene killing my uncle Dominick. Besides, since my father ran good restaurants, paid his taxes from his businesses and went to work just like everybody else, there was no need to reveal his other career. What would be the point? This was my father's unique world, and certainly not mine.

There is one story about gambling I remember with details. My father's gambling associates sent him to the Atlantic City Racetrack to legitimately wager about $25,000 on a certain horse. He was to gradually bet all of that money over time and well before the designated race so the pari-mutuel odds would not noticeably drop. That horse was going to win because the race had been fixed. Several jockeys were in on the fix and perhaps some of the trainers too. In exchange for doing this, the syndicate gave my father traveling expenses and let him gamble a few thousand dollars of his own money. His gambling associates told him to be sure to keep the betting tickets just in case something went wrong and the horse somehow lost. This arrangement made sure my father didn't ignore the directions and got involved in a "double-cross." Of course, the best evidence everything had worked out successfully would be my father returning with all of the winnings, and those tickets would have been turned in at the betting windows.

My father did as he was told, spreading the bets over a long period of time before the race. When the race started everything seemed to be going according to plan. The horse ordained to win was moving nicely running in second or third, moving rapidly into the lead as the horses came around the homestretch turn. Of course unknown to most others, the other involved jockeys were holding back the other horses. From all appearances, the race was authentically competitive and totally legitimate. The horse had moved into first when suddenly, perhaps 75 yards from the finish it stumbled almost imperceptibly, losing some of its momentum – and the race. The fix was in, everything was arranged, but the horse didn't cooperate; it barely came in second. A sure thing turned out not to be so sure. When my father returned to Brooklyn he produced the losing betting tickets, proving that he'd carried out his orders. Because of an accidental quirk in a fixed race, the syndicate lost a considerable amount of money, and so had my father. As Socrates had said, "It is part of the probability that the improbable takes place."

By now, it's obviously clear that my father learned his values and standards from his experiences on the streets of New York, being in World War I and relying on his lifetime political and neighborhood connections. As Leonard Bernstein says in "West Side Story," he was a complete "product of his environment." He had learned that you needed connections and assistance from the people within the various power structures. He always said, "there's nothing wrong with asking, all you can be told is no." But he always hoped to get "yes." And as I noted earlier, he knew that everyone has a price.

My father also learned things by reading, especially newspapers. He often read the *Daily Mirror* because it covered horseracing entries, and the *New York Journal American.* He subscribed to *The Reader's Digest* and would often quote some of the articles to us. He was not as avid or varied a reader as my mother, but I still have some of the books he read, including Dale Carnegie's *How to Win Friends and Influence People,* Vance Packard's The *Hidden Persuaders* and his other critical writings about America. Inside his copy of *The Trouble-Makers* by Arnold Forster he had written, "Best wishes, To Frank Muzio from Frank Muzio, July 10, 1952" in his flowery script. For years he used a beautifully crafted sterling silver Waterman fountain pen. Years later when I was working at Hunter College, I was running down the street and that pen fell out of my shirt pocket. It was gone. I wondered whether whoever found it knew its real worth or considered its history.

My father enjoyed watching Bishop Fulton J. Sheen; a leading and well-respected Catholic spokesperson whose television show was called "Life is Worth Living." The bishop was charismatic and spoke with humor and insight on behavior, character, thinking, religion and moral law. We all had to be quiet when Bishop Sheen was on; we were encouraged to watch him and pay careful attention to his weekly speeches that went well beyond the catechism lessons I'd had as a young child. I recently discovered that a cable television station shows re-runs of Bishop Sheen's programs. My father also watched Milton Berle as an extraordinary comic whose program was sponsored by Texaco. Another favorite was Jimmy Durante, who came from my father's neighborhood in New York, and who my father knew.

During World War II when Maria and I were young children living in Sunnyside, Queens, our father sometimes brought home horsemeat for my mother to cook, but luckily not too often. Even though it was wartime, he ran restaurants and had access to plenty of fresh and leftover food. But he'd still bring us horsemeat, something he certainly did not serve in his restaurants, I don't think. The meat was tough and stringy and had a distinctive odor that hung in the air for days. As we were eating, he would somehow find a way to recount his World War I army experiences almost 30 years before when he'd killed horses and cooked their meat. These tales hardly made us want to finish our dinner, but finish it we did. Sometimes it was my job to wash the dishes the nights we had horsemeat, and I don't think I'll ever forget the distinct darkened ring, often with clinging meat fragments, inside the pot the meat had been cooked in. It took extra rubbing effort and additional Brillo steel wool to remove it.

My mother never forgot the hard work she had to do as a child and young adult, and this must have made her believe that her children needed to do chores at home. On alternating nights, Maria and I had to set the table, clear it after dinner, wash, dry and put away all dishes and silverware. Her assigned nights were Monday, Wednesday and Friday; mine were Tuesday, Thursday and Saturday. Maria needed Saturday nights in case she was going out, whereas I usually studied. Mother took care of Sundays with my father's help and when other family members and friends joined us then. We were allowed to swap nights if we had a sound explanation, but we had to clear it with my mother. We also did some of the food shopping, working from lists prepared by our parents. Every Saturday morning I had to vacuum the entire apartment or house. We sometimes got added chores, such as window cleaning.

In our case, it was my mother who served as the final inspector, not the owner of the Baxter Street tenement she'd had to clean with her sister Lucille. There were no excuses. In fairness, my mother held a full time job, sometimes working six days a week, and we children had to do some of the chores. My parents took on more of the chores once Maria got married and I was at college.

My father always kept busy around the house. He would cook excellent meals, help to clean up (he taught me the proper way to vacuum floors and wash dishes). He didn't have to be asked or told to do chores, he just did them. He also never hesitated to try to fix things in the house or car. Even if he lacked the knowledge or the proper tools, he would persevere; nothing ever stood in his way. He would attack the problem with the same determination, quickness and ferocity he showed with just everything in his life.

As a business owner, my father also had to deal with the unanticipated situations one encounters in the restaurant business. Equipment would break down, a stove, a sink, a refrigerator, even a cash register, sometimes occurred during the busiest times of the day, what were called the "rush hours." So rather than wait for a repairman, he would take care of the problem, at least temporarily, or figure out a way to work around it.

I was never as persistent, and I decided that my father kept at things because of his apprenticeship as a blacksmith and the problem solving he learned as a wagoner in World War I, having to care for the horses and their gear. It's said that people from Calabria are extremely stubborn, driven individuals. The word in Italian is "testadura," or "capotosta" (hard-head). When anyone uses these words, they always tap a closed fist against the side of their head.

Lois and I visited Italy recently with our friends Rose and Michael Mahoney. As we traveled through beautiful

Calabria, people would ask me in Italian where my parents came from. When I replied, "Calabria," the questioner would invariably smile, hit the side of his head and say the magic word, "testadura" or "capotosta." And they didn't even know me!

Over the years I've noticed that our three sons, Frank, Edward and Matthew, share some traits of my father. They are all self-starters and without pretenses or airs. Each of them has preferred to do it solo, resolving their career problems and interests on their own. They frequently avoid belonging to a larger, more conforming network or formal employment. I suspect that, like their grandfather, they want to run things, to be in charge, not be beholden to others or under another someone's boot. I attribute these similarities as demonstrations of not as yet understood transfer of some genetic predispositions in their DNA code sequences. He was a fine father, at least in my eyes, and in so many ways I subscribed to his parenting methods, and maybe that is another part of the answer about our children. Nor am I denying that I have a number of traits similar to my father.

What if my father hadn't been thrown on the streets after the sixth grade? What if he hadn't been a blacksmith, then a wagoner? What if he hadn't wanted to own a restaurant in Manhattan after the war? What if he wasn't a bookmaker? What would have been an appropriate career for him? Well, I believe he would have been a fine teacher.

He liked to tell stories, and I've tried to tell some of those stories here. He had a keen sense of humor when things were not going well. He had a way with words in describing things and loved explaining in great detail how to do something, sometimes drawing a picture to help. He liked to analyze situations and problems. Despite his limited schooling, he was gifted in other ways. He could do arithmetic calculations quickly in his head, he wrote beautifully, and he could play the piano quite well though he'd had no formal training whatsoever.

He also had high expectations, he wanted to do things well and he encouraged everyone – especially his children – to have high expectations as well. He always reminded us not to settle for less or to sell out. He told us "always be yourself," be who you are, not develop pretenses or take on false airs. He talked directly with anybody, right up front. He was a strong believer in fighting for your rights, not letting anyone step on you, and speaking up against any wrong or injustice. He was committed to treating people fairly and decently. He was always interested in meeting and getting to know my friends and wanted them to know him, too. He was a pure self-starter who approached every problem with great energy. When things did not go well, he had an intrinsic resiliency to bounce back from a situation.

When my father taught me to do things he thought I needed to know he did so by example, first doing it and then letting me do it until I could do it well. For example, he believed it was better to take care of one's clothes than to send them to the cleaners; you would save money and the clothes would last longer. So he taught me how to spot clean trousers and jackets then press them using a tailor's pressing cloth and showed me how to iron my shirts and trousers. He also taught me how to sew buttons on shirts, mend tears and make other repairs. He explained to me the importance of using wooden shoetrees to preserve your leather shoes and their shape, and how the wood absorbed any odors. All of these practical lessons saved money and time, and made me less dependent on others. Later, when I was at college and especially in the Marine Corps, my buddies were amazed at how well I took care of my clothing and military gear. Sometimes they'd ask for assistance and I gave it happily, saving them from constantly sending their clothes expensively to the cleaner or tailor near the campus or base.

When my facial hair started growing, my father gave me extensive shaving lessons. As in so many other situations, he believed in attention to details. He spent time explaining the fine points of getting a good shave using either his pearl-handled straight razor or a Hoffritz double-edged safety razor. And he explained the advantages and disadvantages of both methods. With the double-edged razor, my father told me to always use a fresh blade and tighten the razor head to insure a safe, even cut. He explained the importance of properly sharpening the straight razor properly on the leather strop he'd fastened to the bathroom doorknob. A good shave also required copious amounts of warm water, a good amount of shaving lather, of course, not being in a hurry. My mother's brother brought his own razor strop when he came over to cut my hair. If I were blindfolded, I could still recognize the unique sound of Uncle Dominick moving the razor smoothly and rhythmically across the strop to sharpen it.

After showing me the proper techniques, my father turned me loose to experiment while carefully watching and commenting. After nicking my face a few times, I finally got the hang of it. I even learned not to shave too close to the moles on my face, which bled profusely if I cut them. I would never have imagined that years later I would need to remember and use these skills when I shaved my father's face when he was ill and dying in the Veteran's Administration hospital.

Even when I was younger my father taught me how to do things without smothering me. In 1944 when I was about 12, the local Boy Scout troop in Sunnyside wanted each scout to plan and build a project related to nature. The Genovese drug store on 45th Street would display the results of this project in its front window to demonstrate our skills. I was getting nervous as the deadline approached and I couldn't come up with any ideas. I used to take long walks and think about what I could do. Finally, I asked my father for ideas. He asked me what I wanted to achieve and we discussed it. The discussion helped me to suddenly in a flash decide to build a huge birdhouse with an original design, big enough for many birds. I wanted to build a log cabin with lots of openings for the birds, using branches that had fallen from trees. At my father's suggestion, I first sketched out my plans on paper.

We went to a local park and gathered up the straightest dead branches we could find. I then used some thin boards to build a basic structure to support the "logs" I would tack on. It took me a long time; every so often my father came into my room to check my progress. He offered suggestions but let me do all the work; this was my project, not his. Finally I built a large log cabin with several windows but no front door or chimney. I attached perches beneath each window. I think it was the largest log cabin birdhouse ever built. It received a lot of attention in the drug store window and I won a ribbon for my work. I wonder whatever happened to that birdhouse and sometimes wish I had kept it; it was sturdy enough to have lasted. But I remember it mostly because it was the result of both my motivation and work coupled with my father's patient guidance and advice.

Soon after the end of World War II in August 1945, my parents (mostly my father) decided to purchase a summer home in Greenwood Lake, New York, an eight-mile lake straddling between New York and New Jersey about 60 miles from our apartment in Sunnyside, Queens. The home was comfortable, with knotty pine walls and a screened porch, a fireplace, several small bedrooms and there was a large patch of woods on one side. It was a long walk down the hill to a small sandy beach on the edge of the clear lake; it seemed longer after swimming and heading back home.

Even though it seemed a long way from Queens, many of our relatives, almost exclusively from my mother's side, regularly and without announcement found their way there on Saturdays. When it started getting dark, my mother felt that she needed to invite them to stay overnight. They never refused. Though the house was comfortable it was small, so my parents deferentially yielded their bed to the guests and slept in the hot unfinished attic. These extended visits got to be such a habit that, when we drove back to Queens, my mother always said she was glad to be going back to work: it would almost be a vacation after all the cooking, cleaning and uncomfortable sleeping she'd endured.

One day, my father got one of his ambitious, impetuous ideas. He decided the property would look even better if we took down some of our trees and grew a smooth lawn. He was convinced he and I could easily accomplish this landscaping task, and when Frank Muzio made up his mind to do something, he would do it, no matter how difficult. After we walked around our property, he determined we needed to remove about 18 trees. I was about 13 or 14, and it was not my position to correct his plan or select which trees to cut down. But it didn't take me long to figure out that the more girth the tree had, the more difficult it would be to cut it down and then remove its extensive root system. It would have been easier to leave the trees or just cut down a few. In some respects, my father was egalitarian and he accepted some of my suggestions to remove a few of the smaller trees.

We marked the trees we planned to take down, and began then the backbreaking labor, using only heavy sharp axes and some large, crosscut saws. This was the hardest work I had ever done. Of course we had no safety goggles, no steel-tipped protective shoes or canvas gloves or protection of any kind. We attacked one tree at a time, hacking away at its base, taking turns using the manual and limited tools we had. We were covered with sweat as we worked. Although we did most of the work on spring and summer weekends, none of those visiting male relatives ever offered to help. Besides, I think my father saw this as a solely father-son enterprise and didn't want to bring others in on it, they would only interfere. Unfortunately, as we worked, we paid no attention to various plants that grew among the trees, plants with many shiny, pointed green leaves. After we worked for hours on a tree, it would eventually fall over. Then we had to cut the tree into piles of wood and leaves.

My father decided that the easiest way to dispose of these leftovers would be to burn them. But in piling up the branches we had also gathered those shiny leaves – which unknowingly to us turned out to be poison ivy. So, here you have a father and his son, shirtless and with sweat all over them, burning branches and poison ivy, with the resulting smoke fumes right by us. We finally got tired and decided to stop. We went inside, washed up and ate the dinner my father prepared. We sat around for a while, and then went to bed early. When we awoke the next day we were itchy and covered with red blotches. We had made a huge mistake and now there was no easy correction to it. My father went to town for calamine lotion, but it did little to slow down or offset the inevitable blistering, fever and overall discomfort. This incident occurred during a vacation week, so we stopped working for a couple days and focused on our self-inflicted wounds. When we finally recovered and started again, we were a lot wiser and stayed away from those shiny leaves, and we stopped burning. This was an unforgettable yet highly beneficial lesson.

Even after we finished cutting down the trees, there was still work to do. We had to use the pick and shovel method to dig around the stumps so we could eventually cut and clear away the roots. It soon became clear that we had no idea how to pull the stumps from the ground. Standing in a hole we'd dug and cutting away all of the root connections seemed like an endless and almost unproductive activity. After spending several hours on one stump, my father realized we'd need help. We were not making the kind of progress he wanted, and he had a low tolerance for uncompleted, drawn-out projects.

Finally, he found a man in town who had a couple of powerful mules and a wagon, and hired him to finish the job. This older, bearded man wore dirty overalls and cap, and he looked exactly like B.O. Plenty from the comic strip "Dick Tracy." and he had terrible body odor to match. It reminded me a little of Miss Adinudzio from my piano lesson days so long ago. His mules also looked dirty and stringy. Each time we had a tree stump or two partially dug out, he'd bring the mules up the hill and connect them to the stump with heavy chains. Then he'd yell some strange signal, whistle and the mostly obedient mules would pull with all their strength, digging their hooves into the ground. He'd yell some more, sometimes flicking the reins on their backsides, and after a while, the stump would break free from the earth and be pulled a few feet.

Once we got into a rhythm it took us only a couple weeks to take down all 18 trees. The farmer hauled the debris away with his wagon and mules, and we never again burned the branches or any poison ivy either. We brought in some soil to fill the holes, tamped it down, raked the soil and evenly spread a mixed blend of grass seed, which grew quickly in the sunlight and we soon had a lovely lawn among those remaining trees. These days we might worry about the environmental effect of cutting down so many trees, but there was little thought of that in 1944 or 1945. Once my father decided to clear land for a lawn, nothing was going to stop him. I don't recall once talking about or thinking about what these days is regularly referred to as "environmental impact."

He was equally determined to complete the job when he decided to install a toilet in the basement of our house at 196th street in Flushing Queens. My sister Maria had married Bernie Russell in June 1950, not long before the Korean War was underway. Bernie was in the New York National Guard and expected his unit was going to be called up, that's what they'd been told. At the time, draft eligible men preferred to be active on a strictly part time basis in the Guard, hoping they'd never be called to full time active duty. Because Maria could soon be alone, they reluctantly moved into our house, where they fixed up a tiny but comfortable room in the basement.

One disadvantage of this situation was my mother's habit of going into the basement on Saturday mornings to use the washing machine while Maria and Bernie were still sleeping. By then she'd overcome her habit of putting too much soap into the washing machine, an issue for her when we lived in

159

Sunnyside Queens. But worse, they had no toilet and had to climb two sets of stairs to our only bathroom on the second floor. My father quickly decided to remedy the problem and did it his own way, as he so typically did. He drew up plans, decided where to build, and went to a local plumbing supply store to buy a toilet and sink. The space was far too narrow for a shower or tub; they'd still have to bathe and shower upstairs, but it would be better than it was. My father decided it was important to have at least a small window for ventilation, even though that meant knocking a hole through the thick concrete foundation. He never applied for a permit or worried whether the work would weaken the foundation, or was it being accomplished according to building and health codes.

I thought he'd rent a pneumatic drill and quickly open a hole through the concrete. Instead, he went to work with a short-handled sledgehammer, weighing maybe 5 to 8 pounds and a heavy metal bit multi-grooved at the end. Although it had been years since he was a blacksmith, he applied his still-powerful arms and shoulders to this task with considerable consistent force. After repeated pounding, he finally made a slight break in the concrete. Eventually pieces of broken concrete began flying. As with the tree removal project, he wore no safety goggles, no heavy clothing, and no steel-toed shoes, nothing protective. As the closed-in space got hot, he soon took off his shirt.

One day I heard hammering and banging and went down, to help. After all, I was a healthy 18-year-old football player, in excellent shape. After my father accepted my offer, I started slowly, banging away. It was much harder work than I thought it would be. My arms quickly tired. With no protective goggles I had to close my eyes when chips flew.

But with closed eyes I sometimes missed hitting the head of the bit fully and accidentally struck part of my hand with the sledgehammer. Even when I did hit the bit cleanly, my efforts were considerably weaker than my father's. With slow progress, I soon suggested, perhaps urged that we get a pneumatic drill and some safety gear. My father thought this would cost us valuable demolition time, so we continued taking turns banging away at the foundation. While hammering away, I kept thinking about convicts trying to escape using our technique, and I had to laugh. They would have completed their sentences long before they broke through the prison wall, assuming they'd been undetected by the incessant, pounding noise of the sledgehammer against the bit and concrete.

Eventually and solely because of my father's work, he broke through and cleared out enough space for a metal vent he wanted there. Because he had other things to do, it took him a couple of weeks to finish, but there was no way he would quit. To paraphrase Frank Sinatra's song, "He did it his way." In the end he was proud to show off his accomplishment. He placed a grating/screen over the opening.

Maria and Bernie lived in the basement for about a year while both continued to work at Simon and Schuster Publishing Company in Manhattan. Bernie never got called up for the Korean War, and they eventually found a nice apartment in Astoria, Queens. I'm sure they didn't miss my mother doing the laundry as they tried to sleep, or her other annoying habit of going downstairs at night to turn off their television because she had decided that these two young recently married adults needed a good night's rest and rather than watching television so they'd be better prepared for their work responsibilities. They also needed privacy.

While I was at Columbia, I bought a small English car, a "Standard," it had a British flag hood ornament and a convertible canvas roof. Although he loaned me the $250 to buy the car, my father thought it was a foolish purchase. I guess he wanted me to learn to live with my decisions. I knew virtually nothing about English cars or any other cars, and had not carefully inspected it before buying it. Besides, the car salesman reassured me the car was in tip-top shape. And, though I knew my father knew about cars, I hadn't asked him to inspect it. If I had, I would have learned that the metal floorboards were rusted out and would eventually collapse, dropping my feet and any passenger's right through to the pavement.

When I admitted my foolish mistake, my father offered his advice about installing a new floorboard without even reminding me he'd told me not to buy the car. Although I did most of the work, my father occasionally got under the car to help, as did our next-door neighbor, John Cali. Because his blacksmithing had taught him about working with metal, my father provided invaluable guidance and instructions, again drawing a schematic, though this sometimes meant I had to undo and re-do my work. Eventually I finished. The car was in much better shape. My repair job lasted long enough for me to use the car for one summer, then to sell it, giving me the chance to pay back part of the money I'd borrowed. It took me a while, but I finally paid off my debt. After all, in my father's world, "a deal is a deal." There were days I'd wished I never bought that decaying car, especially when I was initially under it not confident in what I was doing. However, working with my father and Mr. Cali gave me valuable lessons that I still remember, especially the sense of accomplishment my father and I felt when the job was effectively done. He was the mentor, I was the student and we both learned something from this experience, including working together again.

Whenever he was faced with trouble of any sort, my father had a certain serenity about him. Others might be shouting, but he would lower his voice and seek some resolution, usually calming down the situation and others. I benefited from this ability the few times I got into fights at school; I was not really "goody two shoes" my sister claimed. At Junior High School 125, I had several fights with some of my Irish Catholic classmates who made fun of my name, or because my lunch sometimes leaked through my brown paper lunch bag, further proving to them I was "a grease ball." Why else would I have grease on my lunch bag? I could not ignore such hurtful remarks. Afterward, the school would call in my father, who'd leave work to meet with the teachers, usually showing up in his white restaurant uniform and white shoes. My mother's job prevented her appearance, and overall it was better for me. He would listen politely, almost deferentially, and then reprimand me for my poor behavior. This seemed to satisfy the authorities. They must have believed my father was a hard working person doing the best he could with his ill-mannered son, who probably would be take more severe action once we were home.

Sometimes my father's connections helped me get out of trouble. When I was 16, I decided to get a driver's license, even though I wasn't old enough and I knew it was illegal. I got a copy of my birth certificate and had supportive Maria change the date from 1932 to 1930. This was easy for her because she'd had lots of practice modifying the grades on her report card. Now that I was suddenly – but artificially – two years older, I went to the motor vehicle office and got a learner's permit. I was nervous doing this but not nervous enough to just walk away. Some of my friends taught me to drive and I passed the test, becoming an illegally licensed 16-year old driver.

Someone in the neighborhood must have seen me driving, knew I wasn't nearly old enough and reported me to the motor vehicle authorities. After a month or so of driving around, I got a letter ordering me to report for a hearing at the motor vehicle office on Worth Street in Manhattan and to bring substantiating documents with me. I suddenly knew I had created a monster and I was in a state of terror. In one of my few rational moments about this I decided to tell my father what I had done (I was loyal enough to Maria not to implicate her). He was surprised and disappointed, of course, but, as usual, he maintained his calmness under fire. I was sure I would end up in jail for lying and forgery, and would probably never drive again. This was a dreaded time.

He took all the documents, promised he'd look into the matter, and somehow the problem disappeared. He never told me how he did it, but I believe he knew people high up at the motor vehicle bureau. He didn't tell me for several weeks that he had taken care of my problem, so I continued to pray that I wouldn't be shipped off to juvenile jail with serious offenders for an extended period. About a month later he had one of his private chats with me. He sternly warned me to avoid trouble and to recognize the importance of the laws. Don't fool with the authorities, and especially "don't fool with the feds," but that part wasn't fully clear to me at the time. As importantly and relieving, I was still a practicing Catholic, so I confessed my sin, did penance and vigorously tried to avoid getting in trouble again.

Some people might complain that I got special treatment because of my father's connections, and I guess that's true. I suppose that if I had been more ethically sensitive, I would have taken care of this matter more honestly and legally by not letting it happen in the first place. I knew my father's actions were probably not appropriate, but in the final analysis I used him and his methods when I was in trouble. I guess some people might call that hypocritical and self-serving. On any reasonable evaluative scale, both are true.

I later took lessons from a driving school on Queens Boulevard and got a legal license. I was still young and foolish and had several serious car accidents with my father's cars, almost all of them my fault, but none involving alcohol because I didn't drink much. What consistently amazed me was that my father never screamed at me when I called him or returned home after severely damaging one of his vehicles, a couple of them nearly brand new, even though yelling might have been most appropriate. But after each accident his first concern was whether I was all right or if anyone else had been hurt. He understood that a car was just a machine that could be fixed or replaced. Humans couldn't.

The calm, patient way my father handled these crises stayed with me, and I tried to emulate him as we raised our children, especially during their tumultuous teenage years, and they certainly were. Without getting into too much detail about incidents involving alcohol and perhaps more, each of our sons had several serious car accidents, usually in vehicles Lois and I owned. Whenever we received a late-night phone call, I answered by asking, "Where are you and what happened?" Then, just as my father had, I asked if everyone was all right. Once I was reassured that no one was hurt, we'd calmly move on to the clean-up phase. For many years we've lived next door to a fine couple, Kathy and Austin Lowry, and we usually took the cars to Austin's body and fender repair business, which put the cars back into excellent condition. These accidents occurred so often it was as if the cars knew their own way to Austin's shop. I'm pretty sure payments from our insurance company were a big part of his annual earnings. The Lowry's not only live in Leonia; they have a home in Ireland and a condo in Florida.

In early 1957, preparations were underway for the fall wedding of Lois Ann Grant and Joseph Nicholas Muzio. Unfortunately, the plans caused some initially unspoken disagreements between my father and Lois's mother. These were in addition to my being an Italian-American practicing Catholic, which automatically translated to our eventually having many babies. Mrs. Grant, a strong, proud and independent woman, was divorced and did not want her former husband Forest Grant, who lived in Chicago, to pay any of the wedding expenses. However, her limited budget meant we had to limit our guest list. Mrs. Grant believed the Grant and Muzio families should each invite the same number, but that was a major problem for my father. First, the proposed number was far too small for his wide circle of family and friends, and he circuitously offered to help pay for the wedding. In addition, I suspect he did not appreciate being able to play but a minor role in any of the planning, or not being able to call the shots.

In his quest for resolution, he asked my mother to call Mrs. Grant and arrange for them to socially meet, but his prime reason was to somehow introduce this issue and his desires. The meeting took place in early April 1957. Here is the handwritten-in-pencil letter my father sent to my sister Maria and her husband Bernie right after the meeting on April 7, 1957. The grammar and format is strictly my father's without any corrections. The parentheses show my clarification comments for the unknowing reader.

Dear Maria and Bernie,

No interruption I will tell you everything that happened yesterday at General Grant's home. First I want to tell you that last week I wrote a letter to Mr. Charlie Van Doran (a Columbia professor who was a contestant on the $64,000 Television quiz program) asking him to please help me, as I was going on a mission very important. He answered me immediately to tell General Grant my family tree, which I took Mr. Van Doran's advice. Now this is what I told her. Mrs. Grant, my father was a rag picker, looked for rags in ash cans and in fact all my nephew's are still in the rag business. I told how I was always in the restaurant business, only for the past five years I was the head Italian chef at the Waldorf Astoria. (Not true)

I also carved roast beef and turkey at the Turf Restaurant on Broadway, in the window. (Also not true.)

The second step. When Mother and I entered the house, Mrs. Grant, Lois and her sister, who is very pretty, I shook hands click my heels and then I kissed Mrs. Grant's hand. I put on the European act, which went over very big. Of course kissed Lois and sister.

Mrs. Grant's mother was there too, Mrs. Davidson, 80 years old. I kissed her too. They say many of tune is played on an old fiddle.

Well, we sat in the living room, had a Manhattan cocktail with plenty of nice hors' d'ouvre. Maria was the cocktail strong. T & T (meaning TNT, an explosive) only one, two would put you in dreamland. Then we talked and talked some more, then we sat down to have dinner. We arrived at 4:15 PM started to have dinner at 5:40 PM consisting of Roast Beef Baked Potato creamed onion asparagus, coffee with cream cake. Very good. Who carved the Roast Beef, of course you guessed it. The chef from the Waldorf. The beef was like shoe leather. One thing was missing was the beer. Had water. When one eats you drink beer, when you wash your face you use water.

Well we finally left at 8:45 PM. Before I left I gave Mrs. Grant a little sample of my dancing spinned around with her a couple of times and she liked it very much. Then she said why didn't I start that much sooner, it's not fair to tease me when you are leaving.

She didn't mention Joe at all. But her mother did ask us, how we felt about Joe and Lois. Mother and I said we were perfectly happy about it. Mrs. Grant was in the kitchen at the time, in fact she was in there all day, Oh yes, when I left they all kissed me. I am positively, I won her over. I had to win her over for Joe, I looked as sharp as a tack, oh yes, she fixed my bowtie, which she liked very much.

That's the story of Mrs. Callabash (An unknown woman friend that, Jimmy Durante, the comedian used to refer to.)

When are you coming here to help me plant the roses by the fence. I started today had to stop on account of rain, how about Wednesday or Thursday.

Tell that fellow by the name of Bernie Russell if you should run into him, that it will be fine if I see him this November.

Am going to close, Mother is laying on the couch, doesn't feel well, fast asleep.

Then, of course on our way home (from the Grant's) we stopped into Rose's for a few minutes, looking at those sour pusses we left in one half minute. All is well hope that you Bernie and girls (Maria and Bernie were caring for two children of one of Bernie's relatives for a long time) are all well. Kisses to all Bernie too.

Love Good Night Daddy.

Will tell you a secret when I see you. Just for you. Good night.

Yes you guessed it, too bad.

These final remarks undoubtedly refer to my father's unsuccessful attempts to convince Mrs. Grant to let him invite more wedding guests, even though he offered to completely pay for them. I believe Mrs. Grant would never have let this happen, and probably was offended as well. Although he doesn't state his disappointment in the letter, my father did discuss it with us later. It was clear he did not like the outcome, but he abided with Mrs. Grant's emphatic wishes and the balanced number of invited guests.

Lois and I were married at the Congregational Church in Queens Village, Queens on September 21, 1957. By then, my father had been in and out of several hospitals and seemed to be a weaker, thinner man, though we didn't yet know how serious his illness was. He was clearly in pain most of the time, but seldom complained. At the wedding, when I asked him how he felt, he stoically said he was fine, though I could see the grimace behind his faint smile when he said it.

Before the wedding, my relatives urged Lois to carry a large silk purse, perhaps even a pillowcase, to hold the envelopes of money we'd receive from our Italian family and guests. Lois's family had already sent beautiful Waterford crystal, chinaware, sterling silver place settings and other fancy gifts to her mother's house. Lois thought it was primitive to give cash, so she refused to carry a large purse or any kind of sac for the upcoming monetary gifts. But of course, that's exactly what our family and their friends did. As we went from table to table at the reception to visit our guests, many of them handed envelopes to Lois and me. Since she had nothing to hold them, there were no pockets in her borrowed, stunning wedding dress, she stuffed them into the pockets of my rented tuxedo. To this day I'm convinced I dropped some envelopes on the floor of the Amber Lantern on Northern Boulevard in Flushing, where the reception was held.

After we said goodbye to our family and friends at the reception, we changed from our formal wedding clothes and drove into Manhattan in the borrowed Volkswagen. Our dear friends Larry Sullivan and Bob Wilson had paid for a suite of rooms at the Plaza Hotel near Central Park as a wedding present, and up we drove in the Volkswagen. If the car surprised the doorman, he didn't show it, and took it away while the newlyweds checked into the hotel with their luggage.

Once inside the lovely suite of rooms, we ordered chicken salad sandwiches and Champagne. After room service arrived, we changed into our pajamas and sat on the floor, eating and drinking, and opened the many envelopes from the wedding. As we opened and read each card and took out the cash or check, Lois wrote down the names of the givers and simply put a dollar sign next to each name. When I saw this, I told her it wouldn't do. She looked puzzled, and we proceeded to have the first argument of our now possibly six-or- seven-hour-old marriage.

I told her we had to record the exact amount for each person because my father would want to see the list to determine what each person had given us. This way he could compare the amounts we received to what he'd given at weddings and funerals those people had held, and for future instructional purposes when he and my mother were invited to other weddings and funerals. Lois was on the verge of raising her voice, no, she did raise her voice. We argued for a good fifteen minutes and she finally reluctantly agreed to a compromise she structured. She agreed to put the amounts next to the names, but would only hand over this informational list if my father specifically asked for it. I suspect she was hoping to accomplish two things. First, she couldn't believe we were arguing and she wanted it to stop before too long, and second she probably hoped my father would forget to ask by the time we visited my parents from my new military duty station in the Washington, D.C. area. She made one more remark about how primitive this custom was, but there we had little reason to prolong the discussion and we let it drop, for now.

About six weeks later we drove to New York to return the borrowed Volkswagen and pick up our newly repaired VW, and to visit my family and hers. When we pulled up to my parents' house on 196 Street in Flushing Queens, my father came down the front steps, kissed me, and then kissed Lois. Without another word about anything, quickly asked, "Where's the list?" Without public reaction but I suspect raging inside, Lois took it out of her pocketbook and gave it to him. He went into the house and scrutinized it. He was always good at handling and remembering lists of numbers from his bookmaking days. He didn't have to copy the list, he just memorized it, storing in his memory banks for future referral.

To this day, just ask her, Lois still believes I called my father from Washington and reminded him to ask for that list as soon as he saw us. This is totally false, besides that's because she didn't know my father that well. My father needed no reminding, no encouragement or prompting. His actions were built into him almost at the genetic level, and there was no way to stop him from achieving a mission called forth by his Italian-American upbringing, his beliefs and experiences. In some respects, these wedding-related incidents were demonstrative of clashing unfamiliar cultural values. For all of us involved, they were learning experiences, and things worked out despite their initial disturbances.

After we returned to Washington, these generous monetary gifts, plus salaries, sustained us. We bought a few things for our furnished apartment, including a black and white television set, and paid our rent for a few months. Fifty years later, we still have many of the gifts we'd received from Lois's relatives.

My father's health deteriorated rapidly shortly after our wedding and into late 1957, while we were living and working in the Washington, D.C. area. Lois and I often went to New York on weekends to visit my father in a hospital. Before eventually entering VA hospitals he'd been in a couple of other private hospitals because, in typical Italian-American style, my parents relied on a childhood friend, a local hero who'd gone to medical school, Dr. Louis Rosati, but his treatments weren't especially helpful. After my father was transferred to the VA hospital in Northport, my mother, who was working at the Social Security Administration, made the long trip back and forth, sometimes staying with one of her sisters in Queens to cut down on the travel. I remember that she looked confused, drawn and tired, and she could provide little accurate information about my father's condition or care. It probably was the pattern then, medical doctors providing only bare essential information, and my mother respectfully and dutifully not asking questions.

Since I could only visit on weekends, it was difficult to see medical staff at the hospital. After several months of extensive treatment including surgery, radiation and chemotherapy at the VA hospital on Second Avenue in Manhattan, he would never leave that hospital alive. In all that time, though, nobody ever said the word "cancer." There seemed to be a great deal of secrecy about it. It seemed to fit in with many other earlier secrets about my father. My mother asked me if I could get transferred from Washington to be closer to her and my father. She was becoming distraught. My father agreed, and I interpreted this as an outright call for help.

Back at the Explosives Ordnance Disposal School in Indianhead Maryland, where I was in training, I approached the Marine colonel in charge of the program, who raised his voice and assured me since the Marine Corps had selected me for this program, and there was no chance I could transfer out. It would never happen, he said. When I told this to my father the next time I visited him, he gave me detailed instructions on how to make it happen. He told me to make an appointment with Congressman Alfred E. Santangelo (named after Alfred E. Smith, the former Governor of New York State) on a Saturday morning at the representative's office on York Avenue in Manhattan. I was puzzled that I was supposed to meet with the Congressman for the "Silk Stocking District", who didn't represent my father's district in Queens or Long Island. My father just said to tell the Congressman what my problem was, mention Frank Muzio, and ask him for his assistance in getting a transfer closer to New York City.

On a Saturday morning soon after that, I put on my Marine uniform and went to Congressman Santangelo's office on the second floor of a walk-up building. Several people were sitting there, and someone behind a desk asked me what I wanted. After I told him my story, the man told me the Congressman would see me in a little while. When I met Congressman Santangelo, he was looking at the note this man had given him. He asked me if I was Frank Muzio's son, and to send regards to him, he didn't know he was ill. I do not know how my father knew Santangelo, but it must have been from some earlier relationship in the lower Manhattan Democratic organization. The Congressman told me he would look into the matter and would take care of it. I should simply return to my base and say nothing about our visit; things would happen quickly.

Within a week, maybe less, I was standing at attention in front of the colonel who'd told me any transfer was impossible, (he never let me stand at ease). He told me he didn't know what bigwig I knew or what strings had been pulled for me, but I should start packing my bags. My transfer was effective in the next few days. I was going to the New York Naval Shipyard in Brooklyn to serve as the Legal Officer at the Marine base there, which was in charge of security and the brig at the shipyard along with Marine legal matters. My new assignment meant much studying and preparation, but I thanked him, saluted and did a crisp about face. Little did I know when I sought a hardship transfer that I'd end up where my life began.

I told Lois about my transfer that evening, and we were soon driving to Brooklyn through a snowstorm with all our possessions in our car, a German-made Borgwarg wagon. On our first day there we found a small, furnished basement apartment.

Once again, even when he was seriously ill, my father showed me how many things in our country get done through whom you know. It was just another manifestation of his underlying beliefs. In some ways I didn't like the way I got my transfer, but rationalized it as benefiting my parents during a difficult period. Here my father, a man with a sixth-grade education, was able to beat the system that told me my military transfer request would never happen. Though I was conflicted by what someone had done for me and indirectly for my mother and father, I knew enough to write a "thank you" letter to the Congressman for his help.

After my father was transferred to the Veteran's Administration hospital in downtown Manhattan and I was at the Brooklyn Navy Yard, I visited him almost every day. Sgt. Rodriguez, my driver from the Marine base would wait downstairs while I visited. I would make sure I worked later at the base to make up for this privilege, having cleared it with the commanding officer. My father would sometimes ask me what was wrong with him, but in those days no one told cancer patients the truth, at least not in our family. The whole family played along and kept quiet, just as they had when my grandmother was dying from nose cancer. I sometimes thought this denial was cruel to my father, but I never said anything. It was part of this cultural format. How did we ever think this was the right thing to do, this denial of information?

Some days after talking with my father for a while, I would shave him using his favorite shaving cream and a safety razor. Even though he was deteriorating rapidly, he still wanted to look clean and fresh. It's a totally different experience to shave another person, so I was extra cautious. He'd given me my early lessons in proper shaving techniques so I was fully confident in my learned skills. As I shaved him those last few times, I could see that his beautiful facial musculature had shrunken, heightening the square lines of his jaw and along his temples and giving him the look of a person dying of starvation or any other wasting disorder. He was just about finished in his long, painful battle. Toward the end he rarely ate much, his hospital food trays seemed undisturbed, and I knew he was never leaving the VA hospital and going home. It seemed so hopeless. A couple of times when I left, I wanted to return the next time and find that he had stopped suffering. One didn't have to be a licensed medical practitioner to anticipate the ultimate outcome.

He had been seriously ill since early 1956, but even before that deadly cells had begun to secretly ravage his body. In the early 1950s, while I was still at Columbia, he had been diagnosed with tuberculosis and was treated with drugs, primarily Isonizid. But eventually the doctors discovered the lung cancer, while originally focusing on his tuberculosis. There may have been an even earlier factor involved in his lung problems. He once told me his unit had been exposed to poisonous nitrogen mustard gas in France during the Great War. However it's not clear whether the doctors considered this potential damage. And, as I said earlier, for as long as I could remember my father smoked cigarettes day after day.

After he was officially diagnosed with cancer, which consistently remained unspoken about by family members, the doctors took drastic action and removed some lobes from one of his lungs and treated him with radiation and later chemotherapy. None of these treatments worked and they always made him seem sicker. I still sometimes think that this regimen of severe treatments did more to destroy him than to sustain him. This is my polite way of saying the doctors eventually killed him, intentionally or thoughtlessly. He would have died anyway, thanks to his lifetime of cigarette smoking, but I believe the clinicians moved it along with their aggressive and apparently unhealing approaches. Maybe if they'd done nothing except keep him comfortable he might have gotten well enough to return to France and spend whatever time he had left over there. After living there at the end of the Great War, War I, he had never returned.

In the last few weeks before he died in late April 1958, he received shots of morphine or some derivative, perhaps Demerol, to ease his incessant pain. The nurse would often come in, find a place on his shriveled up, bony buttocks and inject the painkiller. But the relief never lasted and sometimes in as little as 15 minutes, he'd say, "Buddy, call the nurse, I'm in deep pain and need a shot." When I went out to nurses at the hallway station, each one would look up from doing chart entries and politely remind me of what I already knew and had been told other times, he'd have to wait a while closer to the designated time for another shot. When he was younger, on the rare occasions when he was hurt, he seemed to have a high tolerance for pain. But those days were long gone. Once he was addicted to cigarettes, now he was addicted to drugs and they provided barely temporary solace. Despite the pain drugs, he was deeper in a narcotized state.

CHAPTER V

THE FAREWELL JOURNEYS

During my final visit with my father, he was in a morphine-induced sleep, probably a coma. This beautiful man had become so emaciated that he looked almost like a small slender boy under his bed covers. I was holding his thin, once powerful hand, watching as his breathing slowed and became so shallow it was almost inaudible or perceptible under the bed linens covering up his chest. Then after a while there was just the silence of the room. I recall hearing the flush of water coming from a bathroom up above his room, no other sounds.

There was no machine monitoring his last minutes, no technological warnings or advanced alerting notice. Nor were there any futile sustaining efforts. I remember putting my face next to his, feeling the stubble on his unshaven cheek and trying to hear or feel breathing. We'd stopped shaving the past week or so. I put my fingers on his slender wrist, seeking a pulse, some feeble indication of any life, but there was none. His eyes looked at nothing, reflected nothing. I tried several times to close his once beautiful, now dull hazel eyes with the tips my fingers but they remained blankly open. After sitting with him alone for ten minutes or so in the soundless room, I began looking for his false teeth. I didn't want others to see his toothless, caved in mouth and lips; he looked too much like the pictures of pathetically emaciated barely alive, weakened Holocaust survivors.

Finally I went to the nurses' station and told them my father had died, he was dead. When a nurse came to his room I told her I couldn't find my father's teeth, but understandably, she didn't focus on this insignificant detail. She called an orderly and, as I walked out of his room, I saw him draw a fresh sheet over my father. His diminutive size was easily fully shrouded. I found a telephone in the lobby and I called my mother to tell her. I can't remember what I said to her or how she reacted to the expected news. I do remember leaving the VA hospital by myself, and going out into the cold air of a Manhattan April night, breathing in dampened air. It was raining lightly.

After my father died we had to begin the sad rituals of planning his expected funeral. It would be strikingly similar to all those he'd attended for so many years, those of his buddies, family members and some others more distant, except this time we were managing the situation. During this period, my mother seemed to be in a state of suspended animation. It took her a long time to reply to any question and she looked both sad and confused.

Maria was especially sad; our father would never see the baby she was carrying. My father was excited about having a first grandchild and had followed Maria's pregnancy carefully, as she had had earlier problems and miscarriages. Whenever Maria would visit our father in the hospital, he made jokes about naming this child. He'd joke that the name "Walter" would be the best one; whenever he'd see Maria, he would ask "How's Walter coming along?" David Owen Russell was born about four months after my father died. He was never named Walter.

When I went to the funeral home in Flushing where my father was going to be laid out, I found my mother in a back display room with one of the conservatively dressed funeral directors, she was choosing a casket. The caskets in position reminded me somehow of how new cars are positioned in a dealership showroom. The man was a well-trained and softly persuasive salesman, and my mother was about to select an elaborate bronze casket. My mother was never good at making such difficult critical decisions, she was hesitant and pensive, and so I asked the salesman to leave us alone for a few minutes. I reminded my mother that my father would have thought it was a terrible waste to choose such an elaborate casket just to put him into the ground. My father used to joke about how much money people wasted on expensive caskets and elaborate flowers; he liked fine things, but he hated waste. My mother chose a less expensive casket, but even that seemed outrageously expensive. I convinced my mother to bury my father in one of his own suits rather than letting the funeral director sell us a cheap one along with the accessories at a high cost. After all, Frank Muzio had been a clotheshorse and his closet was filled with the finest of suits, shirts and ties, most of them from Sulka's in Manhattan.

The wake was a blur as if seen through a shroud of smoke. The funeral parlor had an overwhelmingly sweet smell of flowers, there were floral pieces around his casket and along the walls, and nearby was a small table stacked with mass and condolence cards. There was a prominent crucifix on the coffin. All sorts of visitors spoke to my mother, my pregnant sister and me. I didn't know many of them and have no memory of the words they said, then or now.

The visitors came to pay their respects day and evening. Some of them were old friends of my father's from Manhattan, Brooklyn and Long Island City Queens. On the last night a local priest came and we said prayers as a group. This priest never had met my father, so the words he said seemed programmed, empty and habitually read.

Each time I looked at my father in the open casket I cried. I could see how his long battle with cancer had changed him. He didn't look like the person I'd known and loved. His terribly thin face seemed stretched so tightly against his jawbones. We had never found his teeth, and it looked like there was some sort of athletic mouthpiece protector in his mouth to simulate his missing teeth. It made his lips bulge out and look artificially large. Why was it so important to show everyone he died? My father had always cared so much about how he looked, his appearance, his presence, and this last public exposure seemed thoughtlessly cruel. I would have much preferred a closed casket with some sort of smiling photo of my dad as he had been, but my mother clung to her Italian-American burial traditions.

At the funeral mass at St. Kevin's in Bayside another priest spoke the similarly empty words and clichés of the other priest about a man he never met or knew. This priest mispronounced my father's name three times; they seemed like garbled Italian names, even forgetting his first name at one point. After the mass, we took the long and silent journey to the National Cemetery in Farmingdale, Long Island, riding in black limos, and led by the heavily filled open flower car and hearse vehicles. As we drove we sometimes saw fragments of the floral pieces, a petal here and there, fall from the flower car into the wind and then on to the highway surface. I've never understood the significance of such flowery displays. Yes, florists need income and they provide a traditional service, but what does all of this mean?

At the cemetery, we stood around the hole in the ground near some artificial green felt cover partially hiding the dirt that would be put back in once the casket was lowered after we left. After taps, an Army representative and two other servicemen folded the flag that had covered my father's casket into a neat triangle and handed it to my mother. He said something barely heard. I still have that flag with its 48 stars, and we usually fly it outside our house on July 4th, and, if I remember, on Flag Day and Veteran's Day too.

It took a month or so before my mother was able to talk about my father's long illness, and the months he suffered in the VA hospital. She told me that sometimes men she didn't know would show up at the hospital and hand her a small brown paper bag containing cash. She never asked why or from whom it came; she had long ago accepted my father's tenet, "don't ask no questions" about his business activities. Also, she needed the money and it blended into her frugality model. I never asked her how much money these anonymous men had given her, but it was appreciatively received.

She also told me several months beyond these men had asked her if her son Joseph (me) wanted to join them in their unspecific business ventures. They knew I was an officer in the Marine Corps and someday would return home. My mother said she told them politely "No, thank you, Joseph will be going on in his education once he leaves the service," and this was the end of the discussion. I never knew anything at the time they spoke with her. We never heard or spoke to them again, and I still have no idea who they were. But I have a strong sense of what they did for a living.

Many years later I saw the movie, "The Godfather." In this film, Michael Corleone, played by Al Pacino, is a young Marine Corps captain who becomes deeply immersed in the Corleone mob's illegal business operations after leaving the service. He eventually became the new Godfather after his father died, and the film's two sequels follow Michael's efforts to become a respected and legitimate businessman. Whenever I see these films I remember my mother's brief encounter with these men delivering cash to her, and their discussion with her. I fleetingly wonder what might have happened if somehow my mother had discussed this matter with me and if I had embarked on a life with those men, my father's nameless, never-again-seen colleagues.

I am absolutely certain that if I had joined these men in whatever their businesses they would have been illegal and possibly dangerous. I also am sure that Lois, whom I married in September 1957, would have left me the moment I made any sort of commitment to those men. Unlike Michael Corleone's fictional wife, Kate who suffered first in innocence and silence for years, and then public rebellion, Lois would have been out the door instantly with her belongings and our children. Lois Muzio was no Kate Corleone.

My mother died in 1985, at 82. I was with her less than an hour after my Aunt Rose found her body in her nearby apartment. Rose called me at the college in Brooklyn where I was teaching, telling me in a shaky voice that she thought my mother was dead. That's all I remember from this hurried conversation. I left the college and drove rapidly to Holliswood Queens. There was a police officer there along with a man in civilian clothes, who turned out to be my mother's neighborhood reliable physician, Dr. Klaus Honig. Dr. Honig had been treating my mother for high blood pressure for several years and she trusted him.

My mother had died in the bathroom while preparing for a bath, getting ready for a long bus trip to visit an old friend from her government days, a woman named Miriam who'd worked for the CIA. When I arrived, the water in the tub was still warm. I know this because I put my hand and forearm in the tub, my long-sleeve shirt was soaked. I sat down on the floor of the small bathroom and pulled her into my arms with some difficulty. This was the first dead body I had ever tried to move. There was a quiet beauty about her now. She looked so peaceful; I wanted to believe she was somehow still alive, almost as if she was taking a nap. I remember touching her lovely face and smoothing her thin hair, and looking at the scar now easily visible on the side of her head, the result of that burn accident when she was a baby and dropped into the fireplace.

While on the floor with her, I remembered my mother's gentleness and decency to everyone. She never said anything unkind about anybody, and only did good deeds for so many others, even some she barely knew. I knew there had been times when she'd been thoughtlessly hurt by someone she'd helped, including several family members and long-time friends, but she never lingered on the wounds and keeping her hurt to herself within her feelings and thoughts, she'd move on.

Before my arrival, dear caring Aunt Rose had managed to dress my mother in a housedress, covering the bra and half-slip she wore. Always concerned with modesty and sensitivity, Aunt Rose didn't want anyone, especially a stranger, to see her older sister, her ever close ally, without proper covering.

After holding my mother for five or ten minutes on the bathroom floor, I moved her off of me and straightened out her housedress across her shoulders and chest. Then I waited for I don't know what. I went into the living room where the police, Dr. Honig and Aunt Rose were and tried to comfort Rose, who by now was breathing heavily and sobbing. Rose looked awful, older than she was. She said nothing.

Up until shortly before she died my mother had been in excellent health. She was careful about her diet, swam regularly at the Flushing Y and was involved in many activities. She was constantly on the move, visiting relatives and friends. She also had continued to read a lot. On the day she died, she had an open copy of F. Scott Fitzgerald's *Tender is the Night* sitting on a table. On the Sunday before she died she had driven to our house where a friend, Fred Cicetti was taking a photo of Lois and me in our yard. She asked him to take her picture, too. Unfortunately, Fred had only a single photo plate for the large, old-style camera he was using. We all agreed to take her picture the next time she visited. But that never happened, she was gone.

A few months before she died, my mother had an incident at home, and our son Edward called us at Steve Viederman's birthday party to tell us there was an emergency involving my mother. Lois and I rushed to her apartment in Holliswood Queens from Leonia, and found EMTs with her. My mother insisted she was all right and didn't want to go to the hospital. At first, I thought she was being stubborn but came to realize it was a combination of her pronounced determination and fear to avoid any hospital admission. Lois understood my mother's adamancy, so we signed the EMTs' release and that was it.

Over the years my mother had slowed down somewhat. Her hearing was diminishing and she was worried about losing her capacities. She'd recently written to her long-time doctor in Manhattan, Dr. Henry Schaffeld, expressing her concerns about aging and the fact that she was getting more forgetful. The doctor wrote back, reassuring her she was fine and wasn't becoming senile, something my mother dreaded. In his letter, he expressed some concerns about his own health and told her he also was getting forgetful, but this was a natural phenomenon. Dr. Schaffeld was a special person who took his professional oath and responsibilities quite seriously and had a deep commitment to sound, sensitive medical care as well as spirituality. Those long letters to my mother, many in long hand, which I still have, showed how dedicated he was to his patients.

There's never a good way or a good time to die, but in some respects my mother was lucky for want of a more descriptive term. Even in the later part of her life she had been comfortable and independent. She had avoided long-term illness, admissions to hospitals, surgeries, and all sorts of expensive efforts to prolong life. She dreaded dying, but dreaded even more the possibility of lingering in illness in a hospital, or being in an assisted living facility and eventually a nursing home, confined and helpless. When I was holding her in my arms that day on the bathroom floor I fleetingly thought how she'd avoided the distress of any long-term illness. There'd be no warehousing of Billie Muzio. In pure street jargon, "she'd beaten the rap." Though I was sad about her unexpected death that had robbed me of any last minute opportunity to tell her I loved her deeply, I was somehow glad for her. She'd died as unpredictably as both of her parents those many years ago.

Further reflection allowed me to realize I was with my father when he died, and I was with my mother within an hour after her death. I'll always appreciate the privilege of being close to them when their physical lives ceased. They are still with me. Somebody once said that once your parents are dead, you're nobody's kid anymore. That may be so, but then again, you're always the child of those parents, forever.

Shortly afterwards Aunt Lucille's wonderfully stabile and supportive husband, Uncle Andrew, went with me to a funeral home on Northern Boulevard in Flushing, Queens to make arrangements concerning my mother's body. My mother had told Maria and I she wanted to be cremated, so despite some quiet rumblings and questions from her more devoutly religious relatives, this is what we arranged. I could tell that the funeral home people were a little disappointed at the choice; they even asked us if I wanted my mother embalmed before the cremation, or a complete casket. My answer was emphatically "no." She was cremated the next day in a simple carton.

When I thought about her cremation I had a fleeting thought how much she dreaded fire throughout her life, yet had chosen to have her full body burnt to a package of meager ashes. I also briefly wondered if there was any way she "felt" herself burning and being cremated, as if her sensory nerves could still detect feelings, but I quickly dismissed this from my mind; it was too gruesome a possibility and besides, nothing could be done about it then.

Over the next two evenings, many of my mother's relatives and friends visited Maria and me at my mother's apartment. The apartment was small and it seemed terribly crowded and hot even though it was only late May, so we left the front inner door wide open. My mother's sisters, their children and some of her remaining friends from her days in Flushing and lower Manhattan years ago came to visit. When they said something to me about my mother I wanted to cry, even though they were being kind. Some of my childhood buddies who knew my mother had stopped by, as had a few colleagues from the college. Many of my mother's older and more distant friends sent Mass cards and sympathy cards but never got to the apartment.

Maria decided not to speak at the services in my mother's apartment, but I spoke on both nights. I chose to read "Like the River" by Thomas Wolfe, my favorite American author. I've read this poem at every memorial service at which I've been asked to speak and for a while kept a list of those dead when I had read it. I still remember the names.

> Why are you absent in the night, my love?
> Where are you when the bells ring in the night?
> Now, there are bells again.
> How strange to hear the bells
> In this vast, sleeping city!
> Now, in a million little towns,
> Now in the dark and lonely places of this earth,
> Small bells are ringing out the time!
> O my dark soul,
> My child, my darling, my beloved.
> Where are you now,
> And in what place,
> And in what time?
> Oh, ring, sweet bells above him
> While he sleeps!
> I send my love to you upon those bells.
> Strange time, forever lost,

Forever flowing like the river!
Lost time, lost people, and lost love-
Forever lost!
There's nothing you can hold
There in the river!
There's nothing you can keep
There in the river!
It takes your love, it takes your life,
It takes the great ships going out to sea,
And it takes time,
Dark, delicate time
The little ticking moments of strange time
That count us into death.
Now in the dark,
I hear the passing of dark time,
And all the sad and secret flowing of my life.
All of my thoughts are flowing like the river,
All of my life is passing like the river,
I dream and talk and feel just like the river,
As it flows by me,
By me, to the sea.

One disturbing incident happened during these visiting hours. While many of us sat around, eating, drinking and talking in small clusters, I overheard one relative asking someone about my mother's will. She even spent a few minutes opening hallway closets and checking the contents, looking under some folded linens. How anyone could be so self-centered at such a time was both crass and incomprehensible to me. It reeked of greed. Apparently this person believed my mother had promised something, though I never bothered to ask. It was very upsetting, but I have never discussed it with this relative, and have not spoken to her in many years.

My mother had never prepared a written will. She had only given verbal instructions to Maria and me about what she wanted us to do after she died. At one point she'd sent away $3 for some blank will forms and instructions, and apparently had talked to her lawyer about it. But she was superstitious and thought it was bad luck to prepare a will, that doing so meant she was close to death. She dreaded death and didn't like talking about it. She somehow worried about worms and other organisms devouring her as she lay in a box in the ground, that's why she wanted to be cremated. I tried to give her a biological explanation of death, that it was impossible to feel this natural, biological decomposition process. But it didn't matter; these were her beliefs.

A few years earlier another dear friend of ours, Michael Sohn a ranking lawyer at the firm of Arnold and Porter in Washington, D.C. had taken a leave from his position there to serve as the general counsel for the Federal Trade Commission (FTC). Under the leadership of the FTC Chairman, Mike Pertschuk, one of Mike's major accomplishments as a vigorous and highly competent lawyer was on the national level to require funeral directors to provide carefully itemized bills of the services they offered and rendered. Throughout the country, there had been documented complaints and repeated incidents of terribly costly not clearly itemized funeral expenses. The prevailing pattern of uninformed "buying a pig in a poke" was quite disturbing and surprising to those burying their loved ones. At the time, the FTC served the public interests and worked in behalf of accountability.

Families burying a loved one are incredibly vulnerable, and there was compelling nationwide evidence of funeral home abuses. Sometimes these burial incidents were so expensive they ate up disproportionate family assets. As one can imagine, the various lobbying groups representing the funeral directors and their associations were not especially pleased with the proposals to change the status quo favoring their positions. Thanks to the new ruling, consumers could see the specific items available in the funeral process; and they could choose which ones they wanted or thought they needed rather than merely accepting an unspecified "package" arrangement with a single high price. This was clearly in the interests of the consumers and choice and was demonstrative of how our government can do something effective on behalf of the general public.

When it was time to settle up the bill at the funeral home, Uncle Andrew went with me to provide moral support. Since he wasn't working at his usual job as a sandhog, he had spare time. My father had taught me to look twice at every bill, and I always did; it's amazing how rarely the error I often found was in my favor. So, I carefully read over the itemized bill while the funeral director sat and waited patiently. When I got to a $600 item marked "transportation" I questioned it. The funeral home wanted to charge us for picking up my mother's body in Holliswood and transporting it about two miles to their facility. They had charged us even more to take her body to the crematorium, but that was much further away in distance to Maspeth. When the man assured me the charge was correct, I had little alternative but to pay. I did say however, that if we'd known in advance how much it would cost to have my mother's body moved those two miles, we would have hailed a taxicab and brought her to the funeral home ourselves for maybe ten or twelve dollars, not including a tip. The polite and meticulously dressed funeral director sternly told me that law did not allow a delivery by cab. I guess he did not find my remark amusing, but Uncle Andrew chuckled about it right then and there. Even today my remark still amuses me. But at least we had not wasted money by embalming my mother's body and taken her to the crematorium in an elaborate casket, or buried her in an expensive cemetery plot. This was all in the best keeping of my mother's lifetime of frugality.

Afterwards, Maria and I discussed the distribution of her possessions, deciding what each of us wanted, what we would give to others and what we would dispose of. It was done swiftly and cleanly, with absolutely no differences between us. Maria wanted very little and took less. My mother left 10 bankbooks, half for Maria and half for me. She also had a number of stock holdings and savings bonds, which Maria disposed of so we could pay off any remaining bills and divide the remainder. Maria had obviously learned a few tricks from our father. When she cashed in these stocks and bonds months after our mother died, she verified that our mother was still alive. This was undoubtedly illegal, but nothing ever stood in my sister's way, or my father's. I didn't question this illegal action and no one ever knew about it except Bernie and Lois. As I have mentioned, my mother was both frugal and generous, not only to us but also to her close relatives. In 1962, long before her death, my mother had given Lois and me several thousand dollars to help us buy our house in Leonia New Jersey, which we could never have purchased without her help. She'd given a comparable amount to Maria at that time.

Maria wanted Lois and me to have the magnificent mahogany dining room chest rosewood inlay our parents had owned for as long as I can remember. It was from the beginning of their marriage in 1928, but seems much older. It is a beautiful piece of furniture, with claw and ball feet and decorative carvings. As a boy, one of my chores was to dust this chest on Saturdays, making sure I cleaned the various crevices. When my mother would open the chest doors using the key and get glasses or dishes, it reminded me of the tabernacle on the altar in the church where the Holy Eucharist was kept. As children, Maria and I played under it, tying rope to it legs and pretending we were in a stagecoach going across the country. It now stands in our dining room, and visitors always comment on it, sometimes asking where we got it or how long have we had it. Some people even ask how much it cost, but we never knew and, besides, who cares? Sometimes I just look at its beautiful designs and wooden textures and think about my parents.

One of the other items Maria wanted me to have was a worn tan canvas tote bag that Lois and I had given my mother years ago. It has "Martha's Vineyard" printed on the side of it and a drawing of a dock and some boats in Menemsha, in Chilmark on the island. Inside the bag were several boxes of 35 mm slides, a prayer book of mine from when I was a child, some diaries my mother kept when she traveled, and a neatly arranged package of letters bound with string. There were also some other documents, inside carefully labeled envelopes. This came from my mother's orderly office approaches to documents. I've kept this canvas bag and its contents since then, occasionally reviewing what's in it, though I recently discarded the worn bag, which was musty after 20-plus years in our basement. My prayer book has some discoloration on the cover and a delicate mold on the inside that I've wiped off. The rest of the items show me some of my mother's traits and interests; they are clear examples of her loving and caring. As a child of immigrants, my mother was a saver, a collector who not only saved her money but also saved all sorts of other things from her life memories. It's funny how much can be deciphered from the contents of an old canvas bag.

The bundle of correspondence she'd saved in the bag included many of the letters I'd written to her and my father when I'd been away from home. I had written most of the letters from 1950 on, first as Columbia student and, later as a Marine Corps officer candidate in Virginia and as a young, enthusiastic Second Lieutenant at Camp Pendleton, California. There's even a postcard showing an aerial view of Columbia University that I sent in my first few days at Columbia in the fall 1950, telling my parents, "I've met a bunch of swell guys and new fellows from all over." I always signed with love and sometimes used my childhood family nickname, "Buddy." Attached to the bundle of letters is a note from my mother dated "9/80":

"Dear Joe-
I thought it would be nice for you to read letters you wrote to me and dad in your goals and struggles – Am sure you will enjoy reading them.
Love Mom"

The bag also contained a few photographs of my mother and Aunt Rose as children, and several pictures of our family that Maria had taken at parties in her home in Larchmont. Significantly, my mother kept all newspaper clippings and campaign literature from the time in 1971 that I had run for public office in Leonia, New Jersey along with Tom Ford and Peg Muenstermann. We won that election and were swept into office. Along with Dick Dean who'd been elected the year before on the democratic ticket, Leonia New Jersey had its first Democratic majority in its history. Tom was the Mayor, and Peg, Dick and I were council members. Tom appointed me Police Commissioner, but that's an entire story in itself. This democratic majority was in small ways somewhat similar to Jackie Robinson breaking the color barrier in 1947 and playing for the Brooklyn Dodgers. We'd broken through.

My mother also kept a card Maria and I gave her, dated Christmas 1939. It's a Christmas Spiritual Bouquet with a painting of a young Jesus on the cover. The holiday bouquet enumerates the following: nine Masses, nine Holy Communions, five Visits to Blessed Sacrament, nine Rosaries, 300 Ejaculations and nine Acts. Somehow before giving it to them I decided to add another 0 (in a different ink) to the 300 Ejaculations, making it a much greater 3000. Before you start worrying about 3000 Ejaculations to my parents, I suggest you go immediately to the dictionary and look up this word. It isn't what you might think it is, unless you remember being a devout Catholic. It's a religious term for a short, sudden prayer, a term I had forgotten until I looked it up in the dictionary myself.

One of the carefully marked envelopes contains several graduation announcements for both Lois and Joe and their 1957 wedding announcement, along with other documents. I almost missed seeing a small envelope of about 2 inches by 3 inches with a cancelled 2-cent stamp, dated June 10, 1932, and addressed to Mrs. N. Rebecca, 100 Highland Place, Brooklyn, New York. It's a copy of a birth announcement reading, "It's a Boy." That 8-1/2 pound boy born to Mr. And Mrs. F. Muzio on June 4, 1932, was named Joseph. I was touched to learn that my mother had kept this all these years.

In with the letters was a warm condolence note from Leon M. Goldstein, the president of Kingsborough Community College, a good friend whom I worked with for many years. I must have put it in the canvas bag with other condolence letters after my mother died, including one from Matilda and Mario Cuomo, who lived near my mother in Holliswood and knew her.

There were also two diaries, one marked "Travel-log." Both are journals of her trips to Europe, describing what she did and saw, the weather conditions and her feelings about each day's experiences. Whatever my mother wrote a post card, a diary entry or a letter, she always wrote a brief comment about the weather at the top of the page.

I am sorry to report that I was not with my sister Maria when she'd died in Florida on May 22, 2000. She had been seriously ill with cancer for about three years. Just like our father some 45 years earlier she received all sorts of supposedly comprehensive treatments including surgery. And just like then with our father, I'm not convinced they were in her best health interests. The treatments were so severe and debilitating. For a while she did improve, certain tumors appeared somewhat smaller and she seemed briefly energized.

Besides being an incessant talker, Maria was an incessant cigarette smoker. Despite all my father's warnings to both of us, she started smoking when she was a young teenager and never stopped right up until shortly before she died when she could no longer hold a cigarette. She smoked at least two packs per day, sometimes lighting a cigarette as she put out the previous one—without missing a word. Everything about her had had a rancid tobacco stink, her skin, her clothing and especially her breath. She continued to smoke throughout cancer treatments, no matter how much we all begged her to stop. By then the doctors said nothing. Even in a coma near the end, her hands kept reaching for an imaginary cigarette and putting it to her lips.

In addition to smoking, Maria had become an extremely heavy drinker. It's hard to know when her drinking became so serious, but I would classify her as an alcoholic. Early on when her drinking was less noticeable, she'd walk around with a glass of a clear liquid. She told us it was water, but it turned out to be really vodka. Sometimes when Bernie's job had taken him out of town she would call us from their home in Boca Raton or Larchmont, rambling on the phone with slurred words. It was so difficult to deal with that Lois and I agreed to take turns talking with her. Over the years, Bernie yelled at her just as he did about her smoking, sometimes publicly, and he even hid or threw out bottles of alcohol in the house before he went away on trips.

But no amount of yelling, admonishing or hiding alcohol ever worked to end her addiction. I once wrote Maria a long letter about her drinking, but that didn't work either. Shortly after the letter she drove to Brooklyn from Larchmont and we had lunch at Gargiulo's Restaurant near Coney Island. When she didn't drink at all that day, she pointed this out when we left, using it as her defense against my perceptual distortions. She told me she was fine.

There was a brief hopeful period in the early 1990s when we thought we could make a breakthrough. Bernie, their son David and I met over dinner in Manhattan near Hunter College to discuss Maria's drinking. After much discussion, they reluctantly agreed with my position that we needed an intervention. The matter was beyond easy controls or solutions. Family members would confront Maria directly, and then send her to a clinic to be detoxified and treated. I volunteered to go to Florida and carry out this intervention. It was not a mission I was looking forward to carrying out, but it was a necessary one and she might be saved.

Sadly, that planned intervention never took place. Maria somehow found out about our plan and angrily chastised me in a phone call amidst another drinking episode. She screamed that I had betrayed her, and nothing I said could convince her otherwise. There seems little purpose now to speculate how she uncovered our plan. I believe it was Eldridge Cleaver who said: "an inaction is an action," and that is exactly what happened. Maria continued to follow her self-destructive path, continuing to drink and smoke too much until she could do neither. She died much sooner than was necessary, but she made it all happen; she made choices. While each person is responsible for his or her behavior, I still believe we had failed her.

Even while she was ill, Maria continued using powerful hormonal drugs for a long time to keep her metabolism up and her weight down. When she was younger she was heavier, more similar to our mother. She also began taking estrogen to counteract menopausal symptoms. This was a risky thing for a person with a family history of cancer, but she was willing to take that chance because of how well she felt and because the hormones enhanced her breasts. Lois had warned her long ago about the dangers, but Maria did what she wanted to do. This was her determined, willful personality.

In the year before Maria died, Lois and I had flown to Boca Raton several times, more than we'd visited her in all the years they'd lived in Boca Raton. Edward and Matthew were close to Maria and loved her dearly, and they joined me on one of these belated visits. Our other son Frank was also close to Maria and to David. I have to admit that it was my fault that we hadn't visited Maria and her family more often. Even though Maria urged us to visit her, we didn't make the time, both of us were working and I was reluctant to fly to Florida and used this as an excuse. In retrospect, of course, this was terribly selfish and self-centered.

I also can't explain why I selfishly chose not to attend my nephew David's graduation from Amherst. Up until then, our family had just a few college graduates, me in 1955, Cousin Fran from SUNY Albany in 1966 long after me, and now David. I should have understood how rare and important this event was in our family, but I didn't. Lois wanted to go, urged us to be there, but no, Joe had his way. Upon reflection, I wonder what was I doing and why was I so insensitive about this significant celebratory family event? Later on I found out Maria was hurt by my absence, and she occasionally mentioned it thereafter.

The last time I saw Maria, Edward, Matthew and I visited her in Florida and we went out for dinner. She was so weak that Bernie and I had to help her into their car after carefully guiding her across the street from the restaurant where we'd dined. Once in the car, she looked at me, reached up to where I was standing outside the car and hugged me. Then she brushed her thin hand against my face as I bent over and told me to take care of myself.

Shortly after one of our visits, Bernie sent Lois and me a bundle of doctors' reports about Maria and asked for our opinion. The Miami hospital and physicians had recommended one last, innovative treatment, an experimental gamma gun procedure, something we'd never heard of. The gamma gun would let the doctors more precisely and selectively destroy her malignancies, causing far less damage to those surrounding viable, non-cancerous cells. But Maria's cancer was all over the place. She had metastases in the major lobes of her cerebrum, her brainstem and the cerebellum, which accounted for her seeming to lose balance. Her condition was so hopeless, even this radical newer treatment wouldn't help her. Nothing else was left.

Lois and I studied the reports carefully. Lois had been a registered nurse who kept up with trends in treatments, and I'd been a medical student a long time ago in 1959-1960 and had taught college classes in anatomy and physiology for many years. From the reports, it was quite clear to us— it didn't take a world-class team of oncologists from Sloan Kettering Hospital—Maria was not going to live much longer, it was almost over.

At that point, I wrote a letter to Maria's only son, our nephew David, who was living in California with his wife Janet and son Matthew. Maria and David had a long-term battle of wills, and they seemed to get along only in short bursts. Knowing Maria I can understand some of the difficulties she could create. She related to David in some ways the way she and our mother related with one another. Maria had to make a comment or judgmental remark on whatever David was doing. Even though I hadn't been in touch with David very much, I urged him to fly to Florida to see his mother as soon as possible. I told him she'd be dead in six-to-eight weeks and he needed to spend time with her and let her die believing in his love. Though he never answered me, David did visit and was with his mother for a short time before she lapsed into an irretrievable coma. Shortly beyond those six weeks Maria died with David at her side along with Bernie, their daughter Barbara Jane and Barbara's husband, Joe. I don't know if Barbara Jane and Joe's son Nicholas was there, but he certainly had been on many other occasions and loved Maria deeply. Maria had an especially close relationship with Nicholas.

I later found out after Maria died that David had somehow been able to film those last days of her life. When I found out about this, I was furious about it, and I still don't understand his motives, not that I have to now. In a brief cell-phone conversation, Bernie told me David "was seeking some sort of closure" to the relationship he'd had with his mother. Difficult parent-child relationships seem to have been a pattern in our family, starting with our mother's problems dealing with her mother and Maria's later battles with our mother. But David's apparent need to film his dying mother bothered me. What the hell does "closure" mean? The last time I saw Maria she had specifically told me to make sure no one did anything unusual to her near the end of her life. I reassured her I would, but didn't know exactly what I was pledging. Did I consider David's actions unusual? You bet I did. I was unable to understand the vague and unsatisfying explanations Bernie and David gave me for what I thought was insensitive behavior. David assured me he would never use those films, and I hope he will someday destroy them. I still believe we all need to honor and respect Maria's dying request. How this will occur is uncertain. It's totally out of my hands.

Perhaps I need to be fairer to David, who has a deep commitment to film and its sensitive uses to communicate. David envisions much of life through the camera, he thinks through it, and that may explain his decision to film

Maria. His recent films, "Spanking the Monkey," "Flirting with Disaster," "Three Kings," and most recently "I Heart Huckabees" have made David a sought-after creative director and writer.

Bernie and his children and their mates held a memorial service for Maria in Boca Raton, Florida, where Maria and Bernie had lived for many years and where they had numerous family members, mostly on Bernie's side, along with many friends. But they also had many lifetime friends and family in the tri-state area of New York, New Jersey and Connecticut, so Lois and I suggested holding another service at our home in Leonia, New Jersey, a month or so later, and Bernie gratefully accepted. Choosing our home seemed fitting: our home was her home. Maria and her family had spent many days in this house. She and Bernie had helped us move to Leonia in December 1962, and they worked right along with us to get ready for our first Christmas here. At that time Lois was about six months pregnant with Edward, our second child, and their help was vital. Later on Maria lived in our basement for a while with David and Barbara Jane when they came back from living in San Francisco California and were looking for a new home. After they looked briefly in Leonia, they chose Larchmont in Westchester County and resided there many years.

In addition, Maria didn't attend a church or synagogue and we weren't going to have a memorial service in some cold, unfamiliar funeral home. On Bernie's behalf and for my sister we made calls to many people in the tri-state area from a list Bernie sent us. It was difficult to fulfill this mission, one of those chores that comes up in life and must be effectively accomplished despite some reservations. With each phone call I choked up when I announced Maria's death and the date and time of the memorial service. Some of those I called had not known that Maria had died, and these calls were the most difficult. Lois took care of arranging the furniture and other chores, and I ordered rental chairs and catered food. Although Lois and I and our children were grieving too, we invited only friends of Bernie and Maria and their family, and none of our friends. This bothered me because some of our friends had met Maria and told me they cared about her. The service was for Bernie and his family. Surprisingly, David showed up with four of his friends and film associates whom we'd never met.

On that hot day in June the house was packed with the people Maria loved and cared about, many of whom Lois and I had never met. We'd bought a powerful air conditioner the day before because we were worried about the heat. Lois began the service by welcoming everyone. Then I spoke about my sister in a speech that had taken me several days and many drafts to write. I wanted it to be as perfect as I could make it. I first said how Bernie was a true hero for the way he attended to Maria during her long deteriorating health. I did not hide anything about my sister's incessant smoking and heavy drinking, noting that all of us are flawed in different ways and all of us have parts that are mysterious and inexplicable. But I also spoke about Maria's positive qualities, her intelligence, her forthrightness, her tenacity, her fighting for causes and her many acts of kindness, including some who were thankless of her efforts. David spoke last, and he was visibly shaken when he described his feelings about his mother. Lois then encouraged people to tell us of their recollections about Maria. Several people told us poignant tales of how Maria had helped them; others spoke about how she'd saved them during tough times they'd experienced. There was much love in the room.

In so many ways, Maria had lived a life strikingly similar to our mother's, supportive to others, concerned about other people's welfare and survival. She was another social worker without portfolio, formal training or caseload. She immersed herself in many others' lives. And, just like our father, she could be tough as nails, peculiarly explosive, vindictive, yet also kind, gentle and capable of helping you. Some of the guests showed up even though they'd stopped seeing Maria, mostly because of some kind of dispute, probably provoked on Maria's part. Maria, like the rest of the Muzio tribe, bruised easily and she could be terribly unforgiving, just like her father. But I was pleased that these former friends came that day to mourn her.

Lois created a memorial pamphlet with a collage of photographs of Maria and her family, which we gave to the guests. I saved several copies and occasionally look at them. The booklet was a perfect example of the way Lois does things, tastefully, almost understated. Like my father could, Lois "plays within herself" with a quiet confidence and ease, nothing flashy yet always steady. The service concluded with a recording of Andrea Bocelli singing "Romanza," a piece Bernie wanted to hear. I could hear several people sobbing, and one of them was Bernie. Then, in the best tradition of an Italian-American family, everyone ate, mingled and talked. This was the first and last time I saw most of those people who cared about Maria. Bernie has never mentioned this service, what it meant to him or anything connected with it.

The remains of each of these loved family members were treated in dramatically different concluding ways. My father is buried in the Long Island National Military Cemetery in

Farmingdale, Long Island. His grave number is 5421, section X, bordered by Memorial Drive South and Main Portal Drive. His plain white tombstone is perfectly aligned with all the others and it bears his name and his military title, "Wagoner." I have only visited his grave a couple of times since his interment in 1958, but writing this memoir has made me want to go there again soon. I have a few things I want to think about at his gravesite and plan on saying a few sentences to him, or at least his remains.

My mother was cremated at the Fresh Pond Crematory on May 29, 1985, the day after she died. Several years later, Lois and I took her ashes to Martha's Vineyard and slowly spread them at the edge of the water along a quiet and isolated section of Lobsterville Beach. When we spilled out the ashes from the metal container with her name on it, we saw fragments of small, bleached bones mixed with the softer, flaky white ashes. We watched these remaining particles of her life mingle with the flowers and the gentle breaking of small waves. Eventually they dispersed with the outgoing water. Both of us were quiet for a while, but I cried, and I remember Lois putting her arms around me. Then, we left the beach and disposed of the empty metal container in the trash.

As for my sister Maria's remains, her ashes are at The Boca Raton Mausoleum, Remembrance Chapel, Section K, Niche 5. Since Maria died in May 2000, we've had little communication with Bernie. Over the years it was usually Maria who called or wrote to us, or arranged events with us, so it doesn't surprise me that he rarely contacts us now that Maria is long gone. Bernie's remarried Theresa, a woman he met in Boca Raton. They do a great deal of traveling, and our lives have moved in different directions. On those occasions when we do speak there's cordiality to them.

Despite the years it's been since my mother and father died, they are still with me, as is Maria. There is the unutterable longing for them to be here physically, such a lonely gnawing I cannot express in any language. As my favorite author Thomas Wolfe reminds us in his beautiful and compelling short story "Dark in the Forest, Strange as Time," "there will be silence for us all and silence only, nothing but silence in the end."

CHAPTER VI

THE JOURNEY TO THE OTHER
SIDE OF THE MOUNTAIN

In September 2007 Lois and I celebrated 50 years of marriage. This seems like a hell of a long time, and yet it also seems to have flown by. I keep wondering, "Where did it all go?" What does one say about living with and loving another human being for more than 50 years? How does one comprehend raising our three sons and their life journeys to date? How does one capture those events, feelings and nuances of so long a period? It also seems like a hell of a long time to have lived, 75 years, three quarters of a century. There is no way to encapsulate this time span.

Only recently have humans been able to live as long as we do. It wasn't so long ago that life expectancies were half, even a third of what they are today. We now know that the key factors in lifespan include genetics, diet and where you live. In addition, modern sanitation and medicine including effective inoculations have reduced some powerful risks, and we have clearer knowledge about those dangers in smoking, drinking and other drug addictions.

Many of the relatives and friends who attended our wedding in September 1957 are long gone; only a few are still with us. Both of Lois's parents and obviously mine have all been dead awhile.

And those we care about are dispersed around the country. Our oldest son Frank and his wife Jeanne Bertalami Muzio (I sometimes call her Jeanne Two because there was a Jeanne One, Frank's first wife) live in Rockport, Massachusetts, with their two children, Mia Frank Muzio, now 18, and Joe Grant Muzio (named after me with Lois's maiden name as his middle name) now 8. Mia, Frank's daughter with his first wife, Jeanne McCullough who's home in Vermont, is a freshman at Ithaca College in upstate New York, busy with her classes, field hockey and new surroundings and relationships. Even though she's a freshman, she's playing on the varsity field hockey team. She is a lovely, bright and fine person, with a keen sense of humor, constantly poking at her father.

Frank reminds me of Lois, he is analytical, humorous, and takes on all sorts of responsibilities. I believe he is a fine attorney because he treats his clients with respect and provides thorough professional advice. When Mia's mother left the marriage when Mia was about three years old, Frank raised Mia by himself for several formative years, while actively pursuing his developing legal practice. Frank has been an extraordinary parent for Mia and more recently with Joe Grant, marvelously supported by the second Jeanne in his life, a fine and gifted young woman with a successful career in aviation leasing and purchasing programs, and a large family she remains in almost daily contact.

Our middle son Edward lives closer to us than he has in years. He calls us regularly and usually has dinner with us once a week. We love seeing him. He's living in Saddle Brook, New Jersey, and does electronics installation. He also does construction and electrical work with a contractor. When I am with him I realize how intelligent and sensitive he is. His mind is so analytical and quick, and he is extremely well informed on a variety of topics. He solves problems, plays chess well and is a gifted abstract thinker. Whenever I have something that needs repair or explanation around the house, I call him and he takes care of it. He too has a quick sense of humor, as does Lois. When Edward and Lois joke or banter back and forth, I sometimes am left out because I somehow miss the humor and quips. As they say, it goes right over my head.

Matthew, our youngest son has been in Santa Monica, California for more than five years. He loves living in southern California; it fits his personality. Matthew is full of energy, humorous and direct, and in so many ways reminds me of my father in his ability to pursue things independently and to fight for his rights. He is a gifted athlete who surfs a great deal and works at staying in top physical shape. Lois and I believe he is on the brink of good fortune out there; we shall soon know if we're correct or not. He continues to seek his future in the film industry, he and our nephew David Owen Russell see one another frequently, and have worked together developing projects. He's learned a great deal from his caring cousin. David is already well established in the film industry, and Matthew is just beginning his journey. Matthew keeps Lois and me informed about his continuing efforts, and he remains optimistic about success in film.

The Lois and Joseph Muzio family still gathers for special events, such as our 50th Anniversary party, Mia's high school graduation in June 2007 or vacationing on Martha's Vineyard during the summers. We see the rest of our extended family only rarely since my mother's death in 1985 and my sister's in 2000. Many of them have moved away from the New York area, and those large, noisy family gatherings have just about ceased as each smaller cluster has drawn closer. In recent years, many of our relatives attended my Aunt Rose's 95th birthday party in Bayside, Queens, in October 2005, shortly before Rose moved to assisted living in Ogdensburg, New York. We also gathered at the Tavern on the Green in New York to celebrate the remarriage of Maria's surviving husband, Bernie to Theresa, in June 2004.

Now that my grandmothers Maria Tucci Brancata and Caterina Santa Lucia Muzio, my mother Billie Brancata Muzio and my sister Maria Muzio Russell are gone, Lois Ann Grant Muzio is the remaining matriarch, the woman who leads the family by persuasion and attitude. The men in our family have not been weak, uninvolved, or disconnected, but the women have made the significant household management decisions about major purchases (excluding automobiles), where we lived, vacation plans, social engagements, where the children attended school, and other matters. The men who married Billie, Maria and Lois certainly participated in these decisions, but the women were the more dominating forces. Sometimes these women were so skilled they made their husbands believe they had made the decisions on their own. I don't understand why these arrangements worked so well in these three families, but they did. I recall reading somewhere that most societies are matriarchal, but I do not recall the explanation.

And remember, these women held down full-time jobs for most of their marriages, contributing significantly to the family earnings, while still energetically managing households and childrearing, and in Maria's and Lois's lives, extensive community involvements.

When I was growing up in Brooklyn and Queens, our house was always full of aunts and uncles and cousins. There were dinner parties, poker games, birthday celebrations, anniversary and holiday parties and all sorts of functions bringing families together. My parents were especially close to my mother's three sisters and their husbands, cousin Kathleen, daughter of my father's older brother Joseph, and her husband Henry Buono. Other frequent guests included Dolores and Sidney Teeter, Jean and Bill Loehman, Kitty and Leo Rebecca, my godparents Anna and Tom Balbo, Emma and Victor Valli and many other longtime friends. These relatives and couples were together for picnics, parties, including those with holiday costumes, and all sorts of social activities at our house and theirs. Other than the Loehmans, who were part of the Brooklyn women's clothing empire and lived in Mt. Kisco, the others were primarily lower middle-class and middle-class, like our family.

Before I conclude this memoir I want to return to an earlier topic that connects the beginning and the end of this story, my discovery of my father's life as an illegal bookmaker.

As I mentioned, I learned this in 1951 when I was a freshman at Columbia University. My father and I were watching a Senate hearing and he tried to make me aware of the darker, dishonest conduct of individuals and businesses that is prevalent just about everywhere in our society. My father told me he had learned to see such cynical behavior during his childhood days on the streets of Manhattan, and it shaped the skills he needed to survive in this hostile environment. He learned to receive various favors from the local Democratic Party machine, and that too shaped his life.

For a long time I refused to accept my father's interpretation of human behavior. While I was at Columbia, my mind was on a totally new journey, an intellectual adventure far beyond my home in Bay Ridge Brooklyn or Sunnyside, Queens. I was learning about Aristotle, Plato, Voltaire, Pascal, Rousseau, Bartok, Frank Lloyd Wright, El Greco, Adam Smith and many other great writers, artists and thinkers. This was a new world for me, full of revelations. In some respects, it still bothers me to acknowledge that this person I still love lived in two contradictory worlds, and that one of these worlds goes against the ethical principles, even the lingering Catholic beliefs I have generally lived by.

In his own way my father fought for his beliefs and would not yield. He was forever shaped by the lessons he started learning in the streets of Manhattan after leaving school after the sixth grade. He battled most of his life to sustain himself as a person and as a businessman, and he took unusual routes to success. His family was his primary concern. When he encountered difficulties he coped with them, regardless of whether we ask if he used the most appropriate, ethical or positive methods. Clearly, sometimes he didn't. He fought throughout his life using the only unorthodox techniques he best knew and understood. He was a child of the streets who had a strong capacity to love and to teach his children to survive and achieve. His instruction, involvement and love in my life until he died at an early 67 years of age proved invaluable to me and undoubtedly to my sister.

When I gave thought to all of this, it made me feel that from when my father became an illegal bookmaker after he had been a legal bookmaker at the racetracks, he was behaving hypocritically, living a clandestine life of corruption and illegality while simultaneously professing and living diametrically opposite values and behavior within our family. It also confused me that George Riddock, the carpenter I'd apprenticed with at Queens College, held similarly pessimistic views about dishonesty and corruption in America but lived an impeccably honest life. It was difficult for me to correlate their underlying similar views with their different actions.

Nevertheless, at the time I preferred not to believe that our society and individuals were so cruel and repeatedly dishonest. I certainly did not accept the possibility that all of society's institutions, organizations and governments could be corrupt, especially serving special individuals or groups under the pretense of other values.

CHAPTER VII

THE JOURNEY'S END

WRITING this personal history about my parents has been an enriching and exhausting process. When I first started thinking about this project years ago, before I began writing, I thought it might result in 10, possibly 20 pages about my parents' lives. But their lives were so rich with recollections that it has gone well beyond that; it had to. To me the whole thing has been worthwhile. While it could not have been as exhausting as any expedition to Mount Everest, it has been worth every thought and feeling I examined and wrote about, no matter the effort, and I approach the ending of this project with feelings of joy and exhilaration. It took much time to get here, almost my lifetime.

In some respects I believe I have resurrected my parents to a newer and more open and honest level of appreciation and love with this memoir. I know that this work could never encompass everything in my parents' lives but that never was my purpose. It does bring together my memories of the lives and experiences of Phyllis and Frank Muzio and those of their children Maria and Joseph. I hope that everyone who

reads this highly selective treatment of them will benefit. I
believe I have.

Phyllis and Frank were kind, decent, loving human
beings. I was fortunate to have had them as my parents.
Although their journeys were unique, uneven and perplexing
they easily could be similar to those lives of many parents
throughout the world. They carried out their chores, made
small and important decisions, confronted many problems,
experienced disappointments, including tragic ones, helped
to prepare their children for the society they are in and loved
their children without qualification for as long as they lived.
Again and again, they gave of themselves without complaint
or whining and without expecting rewards. Their reward was
the giving. Beyond these traits, they never blamed anyone
else if and when something untoward occurred in their lives.
They did not offer excuses. Then, like all of us will and must,
they died and are gone forever, except in memories and this
memoir. And, these too will ultimately fade away into silence.

Much remains hidden in the worn fabric of long-past
events and forgotten incidents. I have presented my memories
of Phyllis and Frank as truthfully as I could, and I thank my
few remaining family members for their help in remembering
what they could. I hope there is something valuable here for
others to consider, discuss, dispute and translate. If so, then I
have fulfilled my mission.

If there is any lesson to be learned from this memoir,
it is this: America has been the land of opportunities.
My immigrant parents intensely believed in America, its
freedoms, opportunities, choices and privileges. You could
get here, work hard, play the game, develop more skills
and talents and eventually get a chance or establish one to
succeed. That is what my parents did, and my sister and I

have been the direct beneficiaries of their tribulations and sincere efforts, and so too have our children. As for the future, it is unclear as to what the outcomes will be for all others.

What have I learned from writing this memoir? What took place as I pulled these remembrances of my parents and their children out of my past? In resurrecting these memories, do I have any unfulfilled interests, any unresolved matters? A few. I wish now I had told my parents I loved them. I don't think I ever did this. I did kiss and hug them throughout their lives and wrote the word "love" on birthday and holiday cards, but I don't recall simply saying "I love you" in some intimate moment unencumbered with all the other crowded busy moments.

Also, I could have shown them more gratitude for their lifetime of love and work in my behalf and my sister's, and for all I learned from them. And I wish I had not judged them so harshly for their flaws, their inexplicable inconsistencies or any transgressions I perceived.

To this day, I regret my father's suffering in illness and then dying at a relatively young age of 67. Because of his life addiction to cigarettes and perhaps with some damage from his earlier war experiences, he did this to himself, but I would have preferred he'd been around much longer and in generally good health. That couldn't be. In addition, I wish I had been more forceful and involved in helping my sister as she was destroying herself over the years because of her addictive demons. I could have been a more caring and diligent brother and made stronger efforts to help her save herself so her remaining years could have been healthier, more peaceful and productive.

Another matter I sometimes think about is why I didn't get to know my parents, their inner feelings and thoughts on a whole range of life topics? I've wondered if my sister and I could have been more intimate with them, perhaps we could we have understood them better. It's possible this was too difficult and unachievable because of their upbringing and certain tendencies they had to avoid revealing personal matters about themselves, even to their children. I believe they were not as forthright as they could have been. There's also the possibility they didn't talk much about their intimate thoughts, feelings and beliefs because they didn't know how to express themselves, they were unable to articulate them. Did they believe there was a God or a hereafter? What did they think about their own lives? What were their perceptions about the changes in our society? What were their thoughts about America's future? Why were there things they never spoke about concerning their journeys?

Once I go through such a litany of questions, and upon further reflection, I then ask myself are my expectations about my parents and these various subjects so unrealistic to even attempt to delve into them? What purposes would be served? My favorite author, Thomas Wolfe would tell us if he were here that we are forever alone, we can never truly know another person, and we are always strangers to one another, even within ourselves. It is forever unknowable and lost.

Over the years I have heard many people tell endless tales of woe and disappointment regarding their parents. They complain about how they were brought up and they express irritation and anger about their parents. Some have stopped talking to one or both of their parents. Even years later some of them harbor hostility and resentment about their parents.

It's as if they are rodeo riders who would rather stay on a bucking bull well after it makes sense to jump off. They continue to blame their developmental distortions on what they believe their parents did or didn't do to them. With their parents long gone and unable to tell their side, it's strictly their version, and these people will forever be bound by their negative remembrances and need to assess blame, thereby ignoring their freedoms and choices.

Maybe I was just lucky, not gambler's luck but just plain, accidental, good fortune. Or maybe I was oblivious to what was really going on or somehow chose to forget some things. But in the end, my complaints and disappointments are relatively minimal, and I certainly hold no feelings of any deep-seated anger. This doesn't mean I haven't written about certain incidents and feelings that have made me question what my parents did or what decisions they made, especially when I was young.

As an adult I decided to seek psychotherapy to better understand my thinking and feelings, briefly while in medical school in 1959-1960, and again a couple of years later after I had left medical school. This second time, for a year or so I visited with Dr. Charles G. Carluccio, who was especially valuable by helping me clarify my feelings and distorted beliefs. He guided me to be more analytical, reasonable and tolerant of flaws. He assisted me in becoming a better person.

Recently, after so many years, I contacted him and thanked him for his positive involvement in my life. He seemed surprised I would do this after almost fifty years. We have since met and talked as contemporaries, now two older and more experienced men. How strange and wonderful, so much time gone by and he's still in my life.

I do believe that some of my residual discomfort and awkwardness is related to my parents' decisions, occasional inertia or lack of direction. Even today I sometimes feel an unspoken loneliness, uncertainty, and, by contrast, even an intense combativeness in my daily life. Perhaps this ability to confront issues or people shows a need to verify my worth over and over again, thereby offsetting any perceived shortcomings. Over the years, I've gotten pretty good at building up defenses against certain feelings and I believe that, for the most part, they are less visible to others, especially to those unfamiliar with the impact of my past life.

However, after closely examining my recollections, old family photographs, some of my mother's papers, and considering what my relatives have reminded me of, I still believe I was fortunate. My parents did extremely well by me. Yes, some of the things they did were less than wise, sometimes thoughtless and possibly damaging, and the results still affect me today. But I understand that these were the decisions and actions of parents trying to do their best. And it makes little sense to look back. I just hope I'm not in some sort of long-term denial or amnesic state.

As I've already said, my sister Maria and I were incessant talkers. And we both fought against what we perceived to be the wrongs around us. Over the years I had meant to talk with Maria about these traits we shared, but sadly we never got around to it before she died. But it does seem highly unusual for two children with the same parents to be such chatterboxes. I wonder what went on in our upbringing to promote such non-stop word barrages.

One other trait Maria and I shared was being extremely judgmental of others and ourselves for the things we may have done. We often seemed to have some comment or criticism, some finger pointing, mostly negative on behavioral observations. It's almost as if we saw the flaws without seeing anything positive. While I was attending Queens College, Joan Rosenzweig, a friend and a psychology major, told me she thought I would always be disappointed in life because I expected too much of myself and certainly too much of others. I think she was at least partially correct, though in recent years I have vigorously worked to become more balanced and less harsh with both others and myself. It's a lot easier this way.

When she was criticizing people's behavior, Maria frequently used the Italian word "cazzata " (originally I thought it was "cazzaria" but according to my editor there is no such a term) to describe the stupidity, the nonsense or disorderliness of another person's life. My friend, Dante, who is originally from Calabria and owns an Italian restaurant in Leonia, hinted that the word I pronounced to him is a vulgarity, but he wouldn't tell me what it is. His wife Elena who is from Sicily wasn't specific either, but implied that it has negative connotations. Even though Maria knew but a few Italian words, most of what she knew seemed to be nasty slang or some disparaging connotation. If you didn't know better, you might have thought she'd been born in Italy or had studied Italian. Neither was true, but that didn't stop her. As she got older she looked a lot like our mother did.

I'll never know why Maria and I became so judgmental and critical. Could it have been something in our childhood experience, or some influence from our parents? I wish I'd been able to talk about this with Maria before she died but we never got around to it.

As I hope I've shown here, our parents were not without flaws. As with most humans, those flaws were without malice, perhaps only inadvertent. Yet I still love them deeply and think about them every day. One recurring memory is the smell of the perfume my mother put on before she rushed out of the house to work, catching the Q26 bus from Hollis Court Boulevard to Main Street, Flushing. Sometimes I rode the bus with her on my way to school, looking over her shoulder as she read the New York Times with her gloves on and a small attractive hat on. And I sometimes remember a particular look my father gave me, or something he said or did, especially on those occasions when I sat next to him as he drove us someplace, and we talked. Wherever we were, he had something to say.

THEN AND NOW

Many years have passed since my father's remarks in 1951 about how he believed and experienced the ways things get done in our society behind a facade of honesty and decency. Is America today as corrupt and dysfunctional as he believed it was so long ago? Are we caught up in an epidemic of dishonesty by corporations, other organizations and individuals that inevitably we are all less than we could be? Have my father's experiences become the more prevalent "touchstones" by which our lives are governed and perhaps will eventually be destroyed? Are we all caught up in some unknowing journey of ultimate failure?

In my judgment, things are much worse now than when my parents were young and wrapped up in their lifetime struggles. I believe that dishonesty is more widespread and intense individually, nationally and globally. It permeates almost every institution in our society, no matter what aggregate denials to the contrary. Is this a disturbing perspective? I certainly hope it is. Perhaps if enough of us are aware of this pervasive trend and speak out about it we might be able to slow or stop the steamroller effects. If it continues without significant and effective modifications including new paradigms and fresh mindsets, then the untoward repercussions will inevitably bring us down. I happen to believe our country is in deep trouble in a number of critical areas, although I recognize that some of my downward impressions and pessimism conceivably could be a function of being much older.

As I review the events engulfing us these days, I think it's time for me to drive out to the National Cemetery in Farmingdale, Long Island. It's been many years since I've been there. Once there, I can follow the provided map to locate my father's grave at Section X, grave number 5421, where we buried his remains almost 50 years ago. I will then stand at his gravesite. Even though I know he cannot hear me, I will quietly whisper:

"Dad, it's me, it's your Buddy. Remember how you gave me this childhood name? Did it originally come from your World War I experiences when you called all your fellow soldiers the same intimate name? Dad, I've come to believe you were right on so many matters now that I couldn't believe or understand then. It took me a long time and a great deal of learning. I should not have doubted you, because you would never have lied to me. You were too good a person and you loved me. I was wrong. Please forgive me for doubting you; you saw with clarity, without pretense, and I was blind. You understood life from your experiences, and my experiences then were so minimal. Now I understand."

I'm writing this part of the memoir in October 2007, shortly after our 50th wedding anniversary, on September 21, 2007. Soon many of our family and dear friends will join us for our anniversary party. When we were married so long ago, Lois wore that borrowed wedding gown from a dear friend of my sister's, Bobbie Goldstein, who died of cancer shortly afterwards. Bobbie wanted Lois to wear her dress that wedding day, as if she was reliving her own wedding day. I rented a somewhat uncomfortable "tuxedo" and accessories, along with my buddies who were in the wedding party. We all looked so well dressed and serious that day. Today, Lois has a beautiful evening gown for this occasion and she looks striking in it. I was with her when she selected it and tried it on and had it altered. Somehow she's as beautiful and elegant as she was 50 years ago, and she moves as gracefully as when she was a young dancer. I will wear the formal outfit I own; no more rented ones, those that don't seem to fit. I haven't worn it since Sylvia Kaser and Mike Sohn were married in June 2006 in Washington, D.C.

Yesterday, October 4th, 2007 I picked up that formal suit from the cleaners, where I paid $8.50 for a simple pressing, without any dry-cleaning. Why should anybody care about this? Because, I feel like I've relinquished a tiny fragment of my independence. Instead of pressing the suit myself as my father taught me long ago, and as I've done so many times, I paid the J & S cleaners in Leonia, New Jersey to do it. Whether I relinquish any more of my independence down the road sooner than later on those more important matters remains to be seen.

It is now almost early spring 2008, the clocks have been set ahead to Daylight Savings Time, and despite cold weather alternating with days that tease of spring, there are many hints of springtime newness and hope. Lois has been clearing the leaves left over from the fall in the yard, and now the snowdrops and the crocuses partially obstructed by the layered leaves can squirm upwards from the softening earth with more freedom. In about 51 days, the Muzios leave the Leonia New Jersey community and many dear friends after living here for more than 45 years. We are moving on to our new quarters in Rockport, Massachusetts.

In the military service, when an enlistment is coming to the end, it's referred to as "getting short." Those "getting short" days then get counted and are marked off on the calendar. Well, the Muzios are "getting short."

Finally, when I was a young boy, my mother suggested to my sister Maria and me that we read many books. One of these was Alan Paton's *Cry The Beloved Country*, a powerful and intense book about South Africa and the continuing tragedy and consequences of apartheid. It brought attention to the deplorably unfair and vicious conditions under which blacks existed and died there. This book is as relevant now as it was then, perhaps more so. In Paton's book, when two of the main characters were about to part, one would say, "Go well," the other would respond, "Stay well."

As my old friend and mentor Bob Murphy told me many years ago, *"Things are never the way they seem."* He was so right, then and now—and undoubtedly tomorrow and beyond.

The end ... at least for now.

FURTHER READINGS OF INTEREST

Anybody interested in a deeper understanding of what it is to grow up as an Italian-American should look into these books; Gay Talese is particularly articulate about his experiences in *Honor Thy Father, Unto the Sons*, and portions of *The Gay Talese Reader*. In addition, I recommend *La Storia, Five Centuries of the Italian American Experience* by Jerry Mangione and Ben Morreale. Another excellent reference given to me by my Marine Corps buddy Don Mazzoni is *Beyond the Godfather, Italian-American Writers on the Real Italian American Experience*, edited by A. Kenneth Ciongoli and Jay Parini. Another valuable source is *A Documentary History of the Italian Americans*, edited by Moquin and Van Doren. A while ago Luigi Barzini published *The Italians,* another fine analysis of the Italian people and Italy.

There are many memoirs/personal histories available to the reader: Robert Murphy's *The Body Silent*; Joe Kinneary's *The Good Lord Hates a Coward*; Tim Russert's *Big Russ and Me*; Frank McCourt's *Angela's Ashes* and *'Tis*; *Indignant Heart, A Black Worker's Journal* by Charles Denby; and *Means of Escape* by Philip Caputo are just a few of the more noteworthy ones. W. Ralph Eubanks' *Ever is a Long Time, A Journey into Mississippi's Dark Past* is an especially poignant memoir. Our dear friend Martha Olsen Land recommended this.

I recently read Alfred Lubrano's book, *Limbo: Blue-Collar Roots, White-Collar Dreams*, recommended by Frank Macchiarola, the President of St. Francis College in Brooklyn. Lubrano was an Italian-American who was raised in Brooklyn as a Catholic by his blue-collar father, a bricklayer, and later attended Columbia. If the connections aren't clear, they ought to be. Through interviews and case studies, Lubrano examines those of us brought up in blue-collar families who now live in the white-collar world. He calls us "straddlers" who still struggle with this duality. This book helped me understand and articulate some residual issues of my life.

David Callahan's recent *The Cheating Culture, Why More Americans Are Doing Wrong to Get Ahead* presents a detailed analysis of organizational and individual examples of widespread cheating taking place in our culture, along with concluding ideas to rethink the pervasive unethical activities on personal and collective levels. Callahan believes we are at a critical time in our society and there is much to do, including new and comprehensive social contracts along with changed behaviors to counter what he terms destructive "unfettered capitalism."

If you are interested in better understanding the formidable roles women have played in the development of America, you can read *America's Women: 400 years of Dolls, Drudges, Helpmates and Heroines*, by Gail Collins. Ann Cornelisen's *Women of the Shadows* provides insights and experiences of the women in southern Italy below Naples.

Jules Henry's *Culture Against Man* and Kenan Malik's more recent *Man, Beast and Zombie, What Science Can and*

Cannot Tell Us About Human Nature are both critical books among many for understanding our journey. Norman Corwin wrote *Trivializing America, The Triumph of Mediocrity*. Henry's book written more than 40 years ago and Corwin's about 20 years ago will both provide comparative historical perspectives about what major collective and individual changes have been taking place in our country over time. I also recommend some books about our modern society and its overbearing commitment to military spending: *Our Depleted Society; The Permanent War Economy* and *After Capitalism: From Managerialism to Workplace Economy*, all three by Seymour Melman. Recently, Jared Diamond's *Collapse, How Societies Choose To Fail or Succeed* provides thoughtful analysis from a historical perspective. Ernest Becker's *The Denial of Death* provides insights into this neglected topic of death and how it is treated. Other books of interest include *Habits of the Heart, Individualism and Commitment in American Life* by Robert Bellah, et al.; *Pricing the Priceless Child, The Changing Social Value of Children* by Viviana A. Zelizer. Also, *Revolt Against Regulation, The Rise and Pause of the Consumer Movement* by Michael Pertschuk might interest some of those concerned about protection of consumers.

Printed in the United States
By Bookmasters